As I Liked It

As I Liked It

by

SIR DERMOT DE TRAFFORD
BANT. YRD

*Chris

With warmest regards

Dermot*

The Memoir Club

© Sir Dermot de Trafford 2003

First published in 2003 by
The Memoir Club
Whitworth Hall
Spennymoor
County Durham

All rights reserved.
Unauthorised duplication
contravenes existing laws.

British Library Cataloguing in
Publication Data.
A catalogue record for this book
is available from the
British Library.

ISBN: 1 84104 057 6

Typeset by George Wishart & Associates, Whitley Bay.
Printed by Bookcraft (Bath) Ltd.

To my children and grandchildren who are all directly interested in their antecendants.

Contents

Illustrations	ix
Preface	xiii
Family History	1
Childhood	19
War	40
Schooldays	48
SOAS London University	55
Navy – Turkey	56
Greece	71
Business	81
East-West Trade	96
Immigration	100
Sailing	104
Family Cruise in the Skaggerak	116
Skiing	144
Other Travels – USA	146
South America	147
Japan	148
Formosa	150
The Iberian Peninsula	150
Italy	151
Endpiece	159

Illustrations

Dermot with second wife Xandra (left) and her best friend, Penelope de Laszio (Lady Keith)	xii
Trafford Hall	3
Dermot with Canon Keenan	5
Juanita Stickney	7
Dermot at lunch with the Stickneys in Antigua	8
Bronn's Bay Mill, Antigua	9
Craigdarroch Castle, Canada. Home of Dermot's maternal grandmother, Henrietta Maud Dunsmuir (later Chaplin)	13
Henrietta Maud Dunsmuir	14
Lady Violet de Trafford (née Franklin), Dermot's paternal grandmother	15
Dermot's mother June Chaplin as a baby with her mother	16
Hatley Castle, Canada. Built by Dermot's grandfather, Robert Dunsmuir	17
John Worthy-Chaplin VC, Taku Fort, China	18
Jane de Boulay MBE, sister of Kay de Trafford	21
Rudolf and Kay de Trafford	22
Dermot with his mother, from *The Daily Express*	29
Dermot's mother and father, June and Rudolph de Trafford at Clock House	30

Four generations, Dermot, his father, his son and grandson	31
Dermot and his mother at Clock House with cousin Shane and his mother, Joan Jameson	32
Dermot with Julian Amery at Angmering	32
Dermot with cousin Shane	33
Dermot with cousin Shane fifty years on	33
Dermot as John Bull	35
Dermot as Red Indian	36
Fishing on the Cowichan River	37
Anne Okosi, Dermot's goddaughter	38
Dermot's mother June de Trafford with her 'jaunty cap'	41
Dom Wulstan Phillipson	50
Laura Pandos with Dermot	72
Laura Pandos	73
Dermot's father and Bernard Baruch in Vichy	92
Dermot and colleagues with Cheetah near Lusaka, Zambia	93
Dermot with founder members of Lincolnshire and South Humberside Institute of Directors	94
Dermot receiving the Queen's award from the Duke of Norfolk	94
Dermot speaks at press distribution lunch in Manchester	95
Letter to Dermot from Harold Wilson regarding National Committee for Commonwealth Immigrants	103
Silver Maid	105
Dermot aboard a dragon	106
Orthos	107

Myth of Malham	108
Kayak	109
Lady Barbara Bossom aboard *Silver Maid*	115
Odile	142
Dermot skiing in France	142
Dermot, sons and oldest grandson on skiing holiday	143
Dermot's first wife Patricia	158
Grandchildren, left to right, Laura, Kate, Mark, Toby, Ed, Isabelle, Freddie, Christopher	160

*Dermot with second wife Xandra (left) and her best friend,
Penelope de Laszio (Lady Keith).*

Preface

This is not an autobiography. It excludes details of my family and love life, for which my children, grandchildren and friends may be grateful. It would, in any case, not have made very interesting reading. Moreover, being part of such a large and loving family I do not want to be seen as selecting any one individual for special mention.

I have in my life been fortunate in being surrounded by many beautiful women, among them two wonderful wives, and although I do not want to discuss my relationships with them in any depth, I would like to acknowledge here the great debt of gratitude I owe to my children's stepfather, who has been a great support to them over what have been quite difficult times.

I am writing this before my memory fails completely because some of my experiences I think are historically worth recording and others may simply serve to entertain. It also provides an opportunity to destroy old papers and photographs, which will save my executors a lot of time and trouble. Above all, I suppose this is a way of expressing my gratitude for a life which has been full of interest and variety and not without considerable financial benefit. I have seen numerous young people all but ruin their lives by having too much money too young and I have therefore been fortunate and delighted to have had nine children with whom to share my inherited wealth.

This book is not intended to be a chronological reconstruction of my history, nor is it intended to be a great philosophical work, merely a recollection of some interesting events of my life and some of the people who have played a part in them.

Family History

I AM LUCKY ENOUGH to be able to trace my family back quite a long way. Records of the Traffords start at Randolph who was first Lord of Trafford and died about 1050 following a life, no doubt, of the usual mild rape and pillage interspersed with a little farming. He was succeeded by his son Ralph who in 1080 received the King's piece from Sir Hamo de Massy, Baron of Durham Massy. Ralph had a son Robert who died in 1120 and begat Henry and Richard, who received a lot of land from the Massy family.

In 1457 Sir John Trafford, 15th Lord of Trafford, succeeded his father and records show that he was engaged in heated controversy with one of the Byron family and a Mr Barret of Manchester records the contents of a curious deed shown to him by the late Colonel Chadwick of the Lancashire Militia, the contents of which ran hence;

>In our 4th Edward's fickle days
>A serious quarrel, story says
>Took place near Rochdale, we are told
>Twixt Trafford and a Byron bold
>The cause was this, we understand
>About some privilege of land
>Oliver Chadwick from Chadwick Hall
>On Byron's part that day did fall
>But afterwards it came to pass
>Lord Stanley arbitrator was

> Who fixed it upon this ground
> Traffords should pay full sixty pound
> In holy church of Manchester
> And from this contract not to err
> To Chadwick's heirs to keep them quiet
> And never more to move a riot;
> Ten marks at birthday of St John
> And ten at Martin's day upon
> Each year until the whole was paid
> To be friends again he said

Sir Cecil de Trafford was the son-in-law of Robert Cecil (first Minister of Queen Elizabeth 1st). He became 21st Lord of Trafford on the deaths of his half brothers and having been a devout catholic was placed on the proscribed list of recusants. He showed his sincere attachment to Charles 1st and petitioned the King to accept his services and those of his tenants and retainers.

In 1642 Sir Cecil was denounced as an arch-papist and made prisoner at Manchester prison and then on board a ship at Hull,

> **Ancient Trafford.**
>
> Although Lord Crawford remarked the other day that there was hardly anything in Manchester which went back even a century, Old Trafford, where the fourth Test match is played, recalls an association going back beyond the Conquest, for the family of De Trafford was seated there before William came over, and there remained down to our own times. The family pedigree goes back to Radulphus, who died about 1050, and "had noe surname, as then few of our Saxon nobilitie or gentry had," but, by the time of Henry II. the family charters introduced the name of De Trafford from their ancient estates now engulfed by Manchester.

Trafford Hall.

where he and Sir Thomas Gascoigne were kept under deck for several months without daylight. Somehow he eventually bore seven sons and six daughters and there are portraits hanging in my son's house of him and his sister Cicele who sadly died at the age of sixteen, which is not surprising when you see how tightly her dress is laced!

In 1841 Sir Thomas Joseph Trafford was granted, by Royal Licence, the right for him and his issue to use the name de Trafford instead of Trafford.

The first Baronet of the de Traffords was Thomas who married Mary Annette Talbot and whose father-in-law John Talbot, Earl of Shrewsbury was a great supporter of the eminent Victorian architect Pugin and who commissioned him to design at least two lovely churches still standing in Manchester. Pugin of course went on to design some of the finest parish churches in the country and later collaborated with Sir Charles Barry on the Palace of Westminster. When I visited the All Saints Pugin church in Barton I admired the family chapel and visited the mausoleum below where Henry Whittle, our agent, assured me, 'Don't worry Sir, there's plenty more room!'.

The other Pugin church is St Anne's at Stretford, whose parish priest, Mgr Keegan, encouraged me to stay in the Bishop's room. On one occasion he got Alex Ferguson to join us for dinner, which I thoroughly enjoyed. Sadly I have not been able to accept his invitation to see a football match at Old Trafford. When the LCC Cricket Club required us to release a covenant to them at the end of the 19th century to enable them to put up commercial buildings. I arranged for us not to charge them in return for all family members being made honorary life members, a right of which I made use on a few enjoyable occasions.

The de Traffords and Traffords lived in Trafford Hall, Trafford Park ever since Sir Cecil Trafford, bought the hall (then called

Dermot with Canon Keenan.

Wickleswick Hall) and surrounding estate in the mid-17th century. The estate became known as Trafford Park Estate, and the family lived there until 1896 when my grandfather, Sir Humphrey de Trafford, sold the estate to Trafford Park Estates Limited after the building of the Manchester Ship Canal. The Hall was left empty for many years, and was eventually demolished in the Second World War. The famous Trafford Centre now lies on the land.

As the de Trafford heir, in 1950 I went to Manchester to see the Estate office and remaining properties. I found the secretary working at a stand-up desk and entering everything in rough before entry into the ledgers in copper-plate. The offices were unnecessarily prestigious. After fixing some pensions I subsequently moved the office to a house in Wilmslow. I also negotiated a deal with the Ship Canal Company who had paid a low price for their original purchase but had undertaken to pay us 2% compound interest on its resale, resulting in us getting all the profit.

I gave all our family archives to the Lancashire Record Officer who produced a schedule for me in 1950. These earliest documents referred to Henry, son of Robert, son of Ralph, witnessed by Alastair de Pilkington. The Pilkingtons are today best known as the family who owned the glassworks in St Helens and produced the float glass system of producing plate glass on molten lead. The de Traffords and the Pilkingtons were in frequent contact over the centuries. I suppose they were a good day's ride away from us. Again it seems we can trace the Pilkingtons far further back than Burke can.

My own paternal grandmother, Violet Maud Franklin, was an Edwardian beauty whose family came from Jamaica. The Franklins left the United Kingdom to help establish a new colony in the south of Antigua at the end of the 17th Century. Their

Juanita Stickney.

Dermot at lunch with the Stickneys in Antigua.

sugar mill was marked on some old maps of mine and I subsequently found a fine estate house had been built above the sugar plantation. With the Napoleonic wars their exports of sugar failed and in inauspicious circumstances they moved to Jamaica where the head of family was employed on Customs and Excise business. By a curious chance I discovered that some de Traffords had also settled in Antigua at the head of Goble's Creek where I myself later bought land. They left after their eldest son had gone to Edinburgh to become a doctor. When I was building my house in Antigua there were two young workmen called Franklin and I couldn't help but wonder whether they were cousins of mine as children often took the name of the owner of the plantation. I never knew whether my branch of the Franklins were connected to the American President of the same name but it is unlikely because the Franklin family historian was a bit of a genealogist and I think he would have known.

FAMILY HISTORY 9

Bronn's Bay Mill, Antigua.

My maternal grandmother's family, the Dunsmuirs, of which she was the youngest of thirteen, set out originally from Ayrshire to work for the Hudson's Bay Company who were opening up mines on Nanaimo. John Dunsmuir and his brother-in-law John Brydon, being experienced miners, thought there had to be a rich seam of coal and they staked it out and made an enormous fortune. The history of the family does not make very happy reading. Sons and grandchildren were over-indulged in whisky and the same, sadly, happened to some of the grandsons. A fellow director of mine, Jack Shirley and his wife Juliet, found a history of the Dunsmuir family by Terry Reksten, and kindly bought me a copy. *The Dunsmuir Saga* written by Terry Reksten and published in 1991 describes Robert Dunsmuir as one of the most loved, hated and enigmatic men in British Columbia. The Hon. Robert Dunsmuir MPP was born in 1826 in Scotland and travelled to BC in 1851 with his wife and children. When his uncle, Mr Boyd Gilmour returned to Scotland, Robert was left in sole charge of the Nanaimo mines before devoting his time to prospecting and eventually discovering the now famous Wellington coal mines. In his time in Vancouver Robert Dunsmuir was responsible for the employment of more than 2,000 men.

It also appears that there were even a couple of plays about this infamous family: *The Dunsmuirs: A Promise Kept* (1992) and *The Dunsmuirs: Alone at the Edge* (1991), both by Rod Langley.

My mother's father, Reginald Chaplin, was in the 10th Hussars and was apparently a first class rider both to hounds and playing polo. I am told that on the hunting field he was known as 'Reckless Reggie' and he was certainly known for being very much part of the Melton Mowbray set, which has recently been documented in *The Viceroy's Daughter* by Anne de Courcy, in which a photograph of a dressed-up Reggie appears. Reginald Chaplin met my grandmother when his regiment was stationed in Ireland. His own father, John Worthy-Chaplin, was well known, being one of the earliest Harrovian VCs. I remember he was much embarrassed by a painting which his aunts had done of him putting the Union Flag on top of the Chinese Taku fort beating the Frenchman by a short head.

My Uncle Jacky had a book made for his family with all his letters, which also served as great interest to future Harrovians like myself. Apparently his mother Isobel was a formidable lady who used to go to Hyde Park and wave her black umbrella at communists and others at Marble Arch of whom she didn't approve.

My grandmother had come originally to Dublin at the invitation of her sister, Jessie, who had married Sir Richard Musgrave, whose property down the river became a second home for all of us. Aunt Jessie was a keen bridge player and I'll never forget the spectacle of each grandmother playing with her grandson and nobody was prepared to lose. We went on doubling and re-doubling until Jessie and Shane won the rubber but lost several thousand points.

Sir Richard and Lady Musgrave had two daughters; Joan, who was married to Tommy Jameson and who became one of Ireland's best known painters, and Dorothy, who was a great horse woman, married one of the men who judged at the Dublin Horse Show, Glen Brown and eventually lived at Glanmire, County Cork. It was Glen who mounted me for any occasions when I went out with the UCH (the United Cork Hunts).

Dorothy Musgrave was a fearsome poker player, completely inscrutable and a very valuable teacher. I always loved the story about their house in Glanmire when Glen was going to a wedding in Dublin and the maid leaned out of the bathroom window and said 'Would you be after wanting your teeth Captain?' A very useful and possibly essential addition to his appearance!

Joan had many amusing friends; I particularly remember a very witty columnist of the *Irish Press*, George Furlong who, when asked for his favourite view of Ireland, said it was looking out of the stern porthole of an outward going steamer. There was also classic lunch at the beginning of the war when Joan had her neighbour from Tipperary, Dick Chartris, to lunch with A.E.W. Mason.

Dick: 'What's it like in England during the war?'
Mason: 'Lots of barrage balloons'.
Dick: 'Must be very bad for the hunting'.

Dick: 'I shouldn't be surprised'.

I never see a barrage balloon now without wondering about its effect on the hunting!

Joan's sayings were memorable. My favourite; 'When in London I always stay at the Ritz. I think it's cheaper in the end.' Not after a day's shopping at Bond Street it isn't. She was also fond of advising her contemporaries that, 'One cocktail is a cocktail, two cocktails are two cocktails but three cocktails is drinking'.

Joan's husband Tommy, a brilliant sportsman and wonderful father, could never see why she was amused by the entries in his diary which showed all his cricketing engagements and then on one Saturday 'Marry Joan'…I remember she tried hard to teach me to paint but it soon appeared that I had absolutely no ability. However she taught me the names of all those lovely colours, Raw Sienna, Burnt Umber, and so on, which have stayed with me ever since. Joan and Tommy Jameson had two sons, Shane, who served in the Irish Guards and was a year older than me and Julian to whom I acted as best man when he married a very attractive Cork girl, Ann Dwyer. Several members of the Dwyer family and the Murphys had and still have houses in Ardmore but Aunt Jessie's Rock House was quite the best and I remember terrific games of roof ball (played with a tennis ball) in a yard with three roofs facing it. In the garden of this house Joan had her studio, where I tried and failed to learn to paint.

Craigdarroch Castle, Canada. Home of Dermot's maternal grandmother, Henrietta Maud Dunsmuir (later Chaplin).

Henrietta Maud Dunsmuir.

Lady (Violet) de Trafford (née Franklin), Dermot's paternal grandmother.

Dermot's mother June Chaplin as a baby with her mother.

Hatley Castle, Canada. Built by Dermot's grandfather, Robert Dunsmuir.

John Worthy-Chaplin VC, Taku Fort, China.

Childhood

I HAD THE DISTINCT advantage of being an only child. It seems that way you get far more attention from your parents and there is no competition for love or affection. In an interview some years ago I said that I disliked being an only child and that was the reason why I had a large family myself. In a way I suppose that is true and I think it sometimes can be a very good thing for children to have to accept responsibility for other children and learn to live in tolerance of others.

My father was an undemonstrative man apart from his problem, the family one of tears, but shortly before he died he opened his arms to me and clasped me to his breast. I was very grateful for this proof of his love. He was never into kissing or any other displays of intimacy but I am pleased to say that I have tried to be more demonstrative with my family and luckily my sons are affectionate with their own children.

Sunday lunches were always an occasion where my father was concerned and his chosen guests were frequently two ex-ambassadors and their wives; Charlie Johnson, who beneath the veneer of Eton and the Guards concealed a considerable poetic talent and an ability to translate Seneca from the Latin. His wife, the enchanting Natasha, was from the great Bagration family. Then there was Jim and Elsa Bowker. Elsa was a great friend to my stepmother, visiting her regularly after my father's death. She was also one of the greatest storytellers. My favourite one is of her lunch with the Israeli Ambassador in Istanbul, accompanied by the French representative. The Ambassadress boasted of doing all the cooking, which the Frenchwoman considered inedible. There was a lull in conversation and somebody said, 'There's an angel passing', to which the Frenchwoman replied, 'Catch him and dissect him, we must eat *something*'.

As a strict Catholic I disapproved of my father leaving my mother and remarrying but after I had followed in his footsteps I changed my attitude and accepted his new wife Kay as a member of the family, along with her marvellous sister Jane, three times Mayor of Sandwich (who enlisted the regular help of Lord Salmon of Sandwich to prepare her speeches), and her two lovely nieces in Washington. Kay had an excellent sense of humour; in bed during an earthquake in Agadir when father was not inclined to go down to a safer place, she said, 'What's the use of being warm and comfortable and dead?', and seizing her lipstick and rosary led him downstairs.

Despite having no siblings to entertain me I was extremely fortunate in having two cousins of about the same age but with very different interests. One, Charles Jessel, lived in Kent and the other, Shane Jameson, in Waterford.

During the war the Jessel house was an open house to my mother and me. We could, and did, go there at any time and inevitably my cousin Charles and I became very close. As children we often rode together and were active participants in the local pony club gymkhanas but most of our time together was taken up with preparing sketches to perform for the adults. I still remember the Stanley Holloway monologues which have since helped me entertain many a bored child on a long car journey. Charles came up to Oxford with me after the war and, together with me and Frank Berendt, was responsible for the refoundation of the Oxford Carlton Club of which Charles, Frank and I all became presidents (a position we shared with the future Prime

Jane de Boulay MBE, sister of Kay de Trafford.

Minister, Margaret Thatcher). Charles still farms in Kent today, where, he says, 'There's nothing between me and the Urals.' To his father George Jessel I owe a very great debt. When it was clear to him that his son Charles was unlikely to follow in his own business footsteps he gave me all the introductions that he would have given to Charles which were of considerable help in my future career. Nepotism has suited me well…

My cousin Shane who lived in County Waterford had a much younger brother so we were lucky enough to share the undivided

Rudolf and Kay de Trafford

attention of his father, a remarkable games player when I was there on holiday. He had played cricket for England, been Army Racquets Champion, and was a brilliant snipe shot, so proved to be quite a satisfactory boyhood hero.

The Jessels and the Jamesons played a significant part in forming my fond childhood memories.

My own family rented the Loder Dower House in Cowfold, Sussex from 1936 to 1939. The Loder Dower House was a lovely Clock House with a beautiful big garden where my cousins and I spent many happy days playing. And as we were not too far from the beach we used to go down to swim at places like Angmering, near Arundel fairly frequently. The house commanded a spectacular view across the South Downs with Chanctonbury Ring on the horizon and a Cistercian monastery which I was allowed to visit (without females of course).

Chanctonbury Ring is a small Iron Age hill fort used in various periods of history and still a notable landmark today. Majestic on the northern edge of the South Downs, the ring stands 783 feet above sea level and overlooks a large portion of the weald below with the old ridgeway across the downs passing just to the south. Its popularity today is not due to the ring itself, but a crown of beech trees planted on top in 1760 by a young man named Charles Goring, an action which at the time rather upset the locals. However, in time the trees were regarded as a thing of beauty, before most of them were blown down during the hurricane of October 1987. The trees have been replanted but the ring, sadly, will not look quite the same for many years.

I remember a most exciting occasion in Sussex when my uncle Jacky Chaplin, who spent his time trying to create and break world records by flying to various cities and back in a day, arrived for the weekend and landed in a field next to our house. Unfortunately he hadn't reckoned that the farmer would let his cows into that field and the cows, thinking the tail of his machine was rather tasty, helped themselves to large bites of it. He couldn't get off as planned on the Monday morning and eventually somebody had to come from nearby Shoreham to mend the tail and he got away the next week, just managing to clear the trees at the end of the field.

Quite a character, Uncle Jacky was loved by everyone. I remember him tending towards quite a phenomenal thirst and once he came into the bar of our club (referred to as the Parson's Rest) and ordering a pint of tomato juice because he was on the wagon. I also remember distinctly a rumour filtering its way back to my Uncle Tommy Jameson about a man on the Roslare ferry from Ireland ordering a dozen bottles of beer, drinking two straight down and putting the rest in his knapsack. On questioning Uncle Jacky admitted that it had in fact been him, 'Yes old man, I was terrified of getting thirsty.' Jacky also did some work for a Canadian Insurance company and one day at the bar he spied Colonel Fred Cripps (Stafford's brother) and suggested life insurance to him. For this he had to arrange a medical and the doctor duly asked him, 'Do you drink, Colonel Cripps?' to which he replied, 'Yes, in moderation. What do you mean?'. Fred went through his average day's consumption, comprising of sherry or champagne before lunch, white and red wine with lunch and brandy and port afterwards. Needless to say, the doctor told him to get out immediately, in no uncertain terms. Fred went on nonetheless to live to a ripe old age.

It was a sad day for everyone when Uncle Jacky eventually departed this earth and his last words to me as he lay dying were, 'I say old boy, I do hope I'm not being a bore'.

My daughter Mary wrote the following memorial poem for him when he died.

> Backgammon player and soldier he
> And generous friend, well-known to Whites,
> But now he is buried beyond the sea
> And will miss the old Celebration Nights;
> And although they will prosper as before,
> When the glasses fill, and companions drink,
> None will expect to see Jack any more,
> But one of them there perhaps will think
> Of a man who wanted his friends to be gay
> And who would not wish us to mourn today

The time at the Clock House was also the period in my life when I started hunting. Admittedly it was only cubbing at that time but it instilled in me a love of hunting which has remained with me forever. Usually taking place in the autumn, cubbing is designed to reduce the number of young foxes and due to the short length of a run a more informal affair and an ideal opportunity to introduce children to the sport. I will never forget those very early mornings getting up in the dark and traipsing down the garden to Pear Tree Corner. In this way I was duly blooded and went on to enjoy some fantastic hunting for the rest of my life.

I only met Sivvie Masters, a one time Master of the Black and Tans once, but I clearly remember the smell of farm paraffin from her exhaust during the tight petrol rationing. Shane told me of the time when she was stuck behind a bus with a lorry coming the other way. She couldn't resist the urge to try and overtake, with inevitably disastrous results. Her only comment after the event was, 'Well it would have been cowardly not to try', a phrase which has been parodied by many of my family ever since.

Later on I kept a pony with my Aunt Vi Menzies who lived at Sherston, which is pretty central to the Beaufort Country. I got very used to jumping stone walls although my pony was not particularly big. My Uncle Keith Menzies (brother of Sir Stuart Menzies, who was rumoured to be either C or M, the head of M16), was quite happy to keep an eye on me but I also remember having a number of pretty girls doing the same thing. I particularly remember Joyce Brassey and June Capel who were neighbours of Aunt Vi. I recollect going to the local point to point, known as Sherston Races, where my uncle, Raymond de Trafford (a man of some notoriety) was also staying. He backed a horse called Daredevil. We all backed a horse called The Wicked

Uncle! Sherston races was always fun with parties on farm carts. Very different to Newmarket.

My Uncle Humphrey with whom we often went to stay at his stud farm near Royston, Herts, was a senior steward of the Jockey Club and I remember staying with him for the start of the Triple Crown which was won by the Agha Khan's horse Bahram, although in the end I actually saw the 2000 Guineas which was at Newmarket, not too far from his house. Uncle Humphrey's ambition was to breed a Derby winner and eventually he managed with Parthia, brother to Alcide who had won the Leger for him quite convincingly the previous year. Parthia subsequently proved to be a lesser horse than Alcide but Uncle Humphrey had fulfilled his ambition nonetheless and the emotional strain reduced him to tears. It was a touching moment. As a family we have always been easily reduced to tears and it is for this reason that I particularly dislike speaking at funerals and similar events.

Uncle Humphrey married Cynthia Cadogan, one of four elder daughters known as the 'Cadogan Square'. The eldest was Mary Marlborough, chatelaine of Blenheim Palace, where I often stayed. Their daughter Caroline was always a particular friend of mine and I remember going to visit her in the nursing home when she had her appendix out. Humphrey enjoyed his cricket very much and for practice he would get one of the farmers' sons to bowl at him, putting a half crown on the stumps, with the promise that he could keep any half crowns he knocked off.

It was at Uncle Humphrey's that I once overheard the most extraordinary conversation on the telephone between Humphrey and Crossman, the owner of the property opposite called Cockernatch. This was at the time when everybody was digging for victory and I heard the words, 'I'll plough up my cricket pitch if you'll plough up your cricket pitch'. In the end it was only

Humphrey's that got ploughed up because the Cockernatch had the reserve county ground.

Then there was Lady Stanley, daughter-in-law of the Earl of Derby with whose stables Humphrey remained in close contact, using the services of their stallions. I have fond memories of the Mills family and the exciting (for me) newt races with Lord Hillingdon's son Charlie, who was about my age.

My godmother, Sadie Rodney, sister-in-law of Leo Amery, had the honour of launching the HMS *Rodney* and, along with her nephew Julian Amery often stayed at the Clock House with us.

However, my very first childhood memories are of staying with my aunt in Victoria, British Columbia and being looked after by my cousin and nanny. I remember being taken to see the 'puff puffs' and from then I have always loved steam trains. I also remember being bitten by a hornet aged three and falling down some steps and embedding a rose thorn in my knee, from which I still have the scars.

Unfortunately in Canada my first experience of Native Americans was rather a negative one as some local natives had stolen some benches from the beach and were therefore not very well regarded by the white Canadian inhabitants.

One of my clearest memories of my early time in Canada is of my cousin Dola's wedding where my younger cousin and I were pages, establishing ourselves under the white damask of the table holding the cake, popping up every and now and then for reinforcements. It was around that time that I was photographed as John Bull for a fancy dress show and as I was fairly tubby then it suited well. I think it was my 3rd birthday party where my aunt had arranged a marvellous centrepiece in the table looking like a forest with moss and stones and so on and with celluloid animals all over it. For many years I kept a celluloid rhinoceros, which is why I still remember the occasion so distinctly.

In Vancouver, where my grandparents built their house, I spent a lot of time with the Labradors and I often say I was brought up with them. My grandfather taught me to fish on Vancouver Island and I remember happy times at the family cabin on the Cowichan River, which had an H. Rider Haggard cutting on the wall. The first visit there I could not wait to try my newly acquired skill of fly casting and before my grandfather had even finished shaving I had hooked a $1^{1}/_{2}$ lb rainbow trout, an achievement proudly recorded at the time.

Tea parties at the house in Vancouver were often well reported in the local press and at big parties you could often find a big teapot at each end of the main table. One memorable report ran, 'Mrs Chaplin poured from both ends'. My grandparents were keen collectors of sets of porcelain in the Gold Dragon design and they possessed beautiful sets in white, black, red and green. My grandmother also had a large collection of Chinese teapots and two highly entertaining Chinese servants Li and Lo and I would watch enraptured as they deftly shovelled their food in with chopsticks. I eventually managed to learn to use them with difficulty and now only attempt it as a matter of pride.

It was also here that I started to learn to play golf. At the end of one of the holes there were a lot of gorse bushes and the Labradors would dive in, emerging with handfuls of balls; one of my essential needs. During the war the golf course was taken over for a naval air station and my Uncle Jacky did frightfully well when the remaining members were handsomely paid off.

My grandfather was also a very keen polo player and there was nothing I enjoyed more than going along with my grandparents to watch the polo. On later visits I used to enjoy walking with my mother through the nearby woods which, sadly, have now completely disappeared.

My grandparents house, Glen Lodge, was built on a slope

A PRETTY PAIR.

THIS is a new and charming photograph of Mrs. Rudolph de Trafford and her little son, Dermot. She is the only daughter of Colonel and Mrs. Reginald Chaplin, and married two years ago the second son of Sir Humphrey de Trafford, the fine old sportsman who knows more about hunting, shooting, coursing, cricket, tennis, and the breeding of horses and dogs than ninety-nine experts out of a hundred in any one of these things.

A charming portrait of Mrs. Rudolph de Trafford with Dermot Humphrey.

Dermot with his mother, from The Daily Express.

Dermot's mother and father, June and Rudolph de Trafford at Clock House.

Four generations, Dermot, his father, his son and grandson.

Dermot and his mother at Clock House with cousin Shane and his mother, Joan Jameson.

Dermot with Julian Amery at Angmering.

Dermot with cousin Shane.

Dermot with cousin Shane fifty years on.

running down to the beach with a very exciting ravine on the left which I was not allowed into unless accompanied. It was on this beach that I was introduced to the unsurpassable American ice-creams. The lawn of the house was the greatest fun and I used to spend hours in a four-wheeled truck running up and down the length of it and on the other side of the sound was Grouse Mountain where people skied in winter. Imagine my grandfather's horror when in his first year at the new house he found four feet of snow outside his front door as a result of a freak snowstorm.

Apart from the *Majestic* and the *Duchess of Athol* we would travel to Canada or America by the *Duchess of Richmond*, the *Duchess of Bedford*, the *Empress of France*, the *Empress of Britain*, the *Queen Mary*, and the *Europa*. Each time involved crossing the Continent by rail on one occasion we attended the Chicago World Fair and we stayed for a couple of nights in the windy city. There were superb things to be seen for a small boy; cowboys and Indians at the World Fair and nearer at the hotel Al Capone and his gang having shootouts. At the time there were not many boys of my age who could boast having seen all the things I had seen and by the time I was eleven years old I had crossed the Atlantic eight times. What I do not remember however is my first crossing to Canada on the Majestic where, according to my mother, we were sitting out in a deckchair with Mr J. Pierpont-Morgan over whom I managed to be sick. Needless to say, since then I have always tried to be more respectful to the rich and powerful!

When I was eleven years old and beginning to feel very grown-up we travelled on the *Queen Mary* to Canada and I dined each night with my mother's lady's maid, Lucie Pialle and I was allowed to choose the menu which they had printed for Mr de Trafford and guest. Most impressive to a self-important eleven year old.

It was around this time that I had my very first contact with

Dermot as John Bull.

Dermot as Red Indian.

Fishing on the Cowichan River.

Anne Okosi, Dermot's goddaughter's wedding. Her father often came to stay in Hampshire.

black people. This contact occurred on the Canadian Pacific Railway crossing Canada where the staff became friends of mine. Almost all the staff were black and became useful allies against my rather strict Nanny. In London after the war I got to know a group of West Indian Catholics and they have remained friends all my life most of them going on to take very responsible positions in Government in the West Indies. One of them became Trinidad's Attorney General, another Solicitor General and another a well respected judge. The judge I have kept closely in touch with, although he has recently retired from the Court of Appeal, and is godfather to my youngest son.

One of the most defining childhood influences on my life and career was my French governess Genevieve Galopin (the name could hardly sound more Parisian). Because I was an only child, she devoted all her time to me and refused to speak English, as a result of which I became a fluent French speaker by the age of eight. Unfortunately I soon also became quite conversant in Parisian slang, not all of which was entirely wholesome, although of course she was unaware of the vulgarity of some of her translations at the time. Needless to say when I subsequently went to school for a year in Switzerland my fear of foreigners, so common to Englishmen, had been eradicated and I did all my studies in French. Inevitably therefore at Harrow I was placed in the Modern Language class. Because of this mixture of early influences I am very much pro-European and regard all the world as my brothers.

My nanny used to give me reading lessons and later on when I could read fluently I used to spend hours sitting up in a tree reading Just William books. Among my other childhood reading essentials were all the Beatrix Potters, AA Milne, *The Wind in the Willows*, *Memoires D'un Ane* and the Dumas books, especially *The Count of Monte Cristo* and *The Three Musketeers*, mostly read in French.

War

I WAS FOURTEEN when war broke out and I remember vividly the Jessel butler calmly approaching the tennis court bearing his silver tray of office to report, 'Air raid warning red, my Lady'.

During the war my mother was attached to a little cottage hospital in Goudhurst as a qualified VAD. She subsequently became a transport officer after the hospital was presented with a smart new ambulance. It was no secret at the time that Dame Beryl Oliver, the rather fearsome head of the Red Cross, disapproved of the jaunty cap my mother wore, but it cannot have affected her performance too adversely as she went on to collect the MBE for running the Petrol Section at Headquarters but mainly for charming successive ministers of fuel and power. No doubt with her jaunty cap.

During the war my Uncle George Jessel decided that we boys should all do something useful on the farm in Kent and started us picking plums, then cherries and then apples. We would pick 28lb trays and I remember working extremely long days. We subsequently became proficient at moving extremely tall ladders (some about 30ft) and of course we had the memorable view of the Battle of Britain from the top of them. One day no less than three planes crashed quite near us. Of course we became great collectors of souvenir pieces of metal.

I remember an exciting day partridge shooting with Uncle George, my cousin Charles, a retired admiral and a young colonel. We had stopped for a peaceful lunch in a farmyard when

Dermot's mother June de Trafford with her 'jaunty cap'.

we suddenly heard the thud thud thud of a plane with engine trouble. As soon as we had identified it as a Messerschmidt 110 we immediately took cover. The services in a loose box, myself in bales of hay and Uncle George and Charles behind a haystack. Unfortunately the plane used this as its centre for circling and effectively chased Uncle George and Charles round the haystack. At that moment a laundry van drew up a little side road and two Tommies with rifles but no battle dress tops said, 'Where did he go?'. So we all piled into the laundry van and drove along to the bottom road where the plane had crashed on somebody's wire raspberry netting and landed on the front lawn. The pilot was marching up and down the lawn, carrying a tiny suitcase with 'München Bahnhof' written on it, while his poor gunner was on the garden bench being attended to by the local ladies. Uncle George's German was not quite up to the occasion when he said, 'Sind Sie der Führer?' when he should have said of course, 'Pilot', which is the same word in English. Anyway the Tommies dealt with the situation saying, 'None of your bloody airs. 'Op in the bloody truck!', and off they went in an army 15cwt which had joined us.

The Jessels used to have a lot of horses around and I inevitably spent a lot of my time there riding. One particular occasion just before I joined the navy, Muriel Jessel's daughter, Vanda Swetenham, drove off with the horse in the milk float to pick up some oats for the other horses. I followed on astride another young horse but unfortunately as we were passing a house I knew well the maid opened the window and as she did so my horse bucked ejecting me on to the ground, head first. As a result I suffered quite severe concussion. It was rather embarrassing because I suddenly had no idea what I was doing with Teddy Swetenham's horse or for that matter, why I was leading his horse round Goudhurst Church! Slightly worried, I practised a little Turkish and, realising by the standard that I must have finished my course, made for home. When I arrived home, I took the saddle and bridle from the horse, entered the rose garden to see my mother and said, 'I think I'm concussed', which of course I was. After a few days in a dark room I was back to normal and luckily so was my memory.

Much of the war was spent with the Jamesons in Waterford. The town of Waterford is built on the banks of the Blackwater and has been a hub or Irish life since St Carthage founded a monastery there in the 12th century. The Jamesons lived in a lovely Georgian house built somewhere above the castle.

In those days in Ireland at the beginning of the war I used to ride the hearse horse, otherwise known as the old cob, for hunts, which served me very well. The West Waterford Hunt was a very friendly one and I knew a lot of the people there, best of all probably Susie Dobbs who lived in a lovely house on the Blackwater which was falling to pieces. She lived there with her mother, the widow of a top civil servant. Susie proved to be a good neighbour, friend and spare girl for dances and trips! Another good friend Anne Hickman and her brother Michael were strong supporters of the West Waterford Hunt and I remember one occasion when Anne was hunting hounds and Michael appeared in a pink coat. Everybody else of course was in black or rat catcher.

One day when I was not hunting, the old cob was brought in to the traces of the hearse with a young hunter. Unfortunately as the hunt came past the young horse made a leap towards the bank. Luckily the coffin stood firm, and afterwards two men were heard to say, 'Lucky he was a sporting man'.

'Who, the corpse?'

'No the father of the corpse.'

But I shall never forget my best hunt with the West Waterford.

I had come over at a weekend and on the Sunday my friend Paddy Walsh took me down a dirty old borreen into a filthy farmyard, inches deep in mud, and we went into a stable, a loose box, where a piece of sacking was pulled off to reveal the most beautiful five year old, so I agreed to hunt him on the following Tuesday if they would bring him to the meet. Imagine my horror therefore the next week to find this beautiful animal in a snaffle. He shot away in the first field and I just managed to rein him back with his fore leg on top of a bank which had a strand of barbed wire along it. After that inauspicious start he got on rather well and we had a very good time.

Paddy Walsh was the man who mounted me for all my West Waterford hunts. He ran a hardware store, did a bit of farming, and was the local undertaker. Late one night a representative of the local band of gypsies came along and after telling him that one of their colleagues, a very big man, had died asked if they could please have a coffin. So he took them out to the shop and they chose the largest coffin they could find but came back half an hour later saying they were very sorry but it wasn't big enough. And then a few days later the place was beginning to smell a bit and Paddy realised that they had left the corpse in his care and he had to give it a Christian burial at his own expense!

One of my best excursions with Paddy was to the race meeting in Tramore. We went with a local doctor and the owner of a glue factory which we visited on the way. Paddy knew all the jockeys well and seemed to be free to enter their changing room at any time. In those days the course disappeared behind a hill on the far side, behind which any reorganisation of places was said to take place. Needless to say Paddy would often emerge from the changing room with a very shrewd idea of who was going to win the next race. This technique made for a very profitable outing.

By the end of the war Shane and many of his friends had joined the Irish Guards and Dick Mulcahy, a local hill farmer, had taken over hounds. We couldn't help admiring him as he would get up and milk all the cows and then bring hounds down to the meet. I remember Ian Villiers Stewart, a former Master of Hounds, complaining that the place had become a 'bloody birdcage' with all the barbed wire.

Another of the famous Dunsmuir sisters, Aunt Emily, at the time was living with her husband Harry Burroughs in a flat in Lismore Castle and he had taken the fishing. Imagine his fury one day when he found Adele Astaire, Charlie Cavendish's wife (and Fred Astaire's sister) who was living in the main house, down on the river with three large salmon lying on the bank. I can just picture his large walrus moustache shaking with indignation and her reply 'It's alright honey, I bought them'. A fact which the Tatler wasn't ever to learn. It was just below there where I caught my first salmon and one of Shane's daughters, Andrea, has since done a painting for me of that stretch of what is known as the Lower Devine.

A man by the name of Johnny O'Brien was ghillie for the Duke of Devonshire and on one particular day, bored with waiting, he made a cast and hooked a salmon. At that moment the Ducal Rolls Royce came rolling down the hill and completely unshaken Johnny came up to the door of the Rolls with the rod in his hand, passed it to the Duke and said 'I have him hooked for you your Grace'. During the Troubles Johnny and Paddy were lying in a ditch proposing to shoot the Duke of Devonshire and when, after some time, he failed to appear Paddy said, 'Sure I hope nothing will have happened to his Grace.' Needless to say they never shot him.

Johnny O'Brien's main centre of retirement was the pub of Widow Feeney in Ballyduff. She was always known as 'The

Widow' and certainly a lot of drink was consumed on her premises. So much so that she was always prepared to write out a fishing licence for us in case the water bailiffs turned up. There is a great story of how the widow's dog killed Johnny's dog and Johnny skinned it and had the pelt made into a waistcoat and every time he passed the widow's dog 'sure didn't the hairs on the waistcoat stand on end!'

I had many friends in Cappoquin, Ballyduff, and one of the best was Mick Sergeant who owned the garage and was a superb fisherman. I remember so well going out with him onto the Blackwater in search of trout and I never touched a thing and he caught about five. Another, a nearby Collinstown farmer called Dooley, had lost his licence for some driving misdemeanour or other and on one particular illegal journey was stopped by the guards with his sheepdog Shushu on his lap. With both paws on the steering wheel Dooley argued that the dog was driving and promptly showed a valid licence in the name of Shushu Dooley. In those days before licence photographs she could have got herself a licence on several West Indian islands.

After the war Shane decided to take up farming full-time but to make it pay he wanted to go into grass drying and this he did with a cousin of his, Dick Musgrave, who was backed by a Northern Irish friend, George McKean, while I backed Shane and became Chairman of Irish Crop Driers. We dried the grass on Dublin Airport and also all round Tourin and gradually expanded until we had four drying stations and the biggest business of its kind in Ireland. I was always terrified at the possibility of one of our more bog based tractor drivers writing off a 707 for which we could not afford insurance. Dick Musgrave was constantly in trouble throughout his life and there is the now infamous occasion when creditors came to the door at our station near the airport and Dick escaped out of the window. Apparently in one of his later incarnations he ended up running shoots for mega rich Americans and got put in jail for killing some sort of protected hawk.

Schooldays

As a small boy I attended a pre prep school, Egerton House, in Dorset Square, London. On sports days I used to take lunch there and the picture of browned meat, badly mashed potato, stained with beetroot is the least pleasant of all my memories but I had great fun making my first stage appearance, nearly, when we did a play called *The Scarlet Coconut* in which I had to be the voice of Paris radio coming from under the table. I think my total contribution was 'Allo, allo, ici Paris' but it was fun nonetheless.

My schooldays proper began in 1934 when I went to Worth Priory prep school. Worth Priory in stands on high land with views over fields and woods and a superb azalea garden. Each boy at the school was encouraged to grow plants in his own small garden and I particularly remember my own modest nasturtiums. The school building was very impressive and the walls were covered with a beautiful deep red coloured satin. The old library was a very grand place and as well as being a place of quiet and scholarly activity also served as a perfect dayroom rugger 'pitch' and it was in the old library that I picked up more than my share of bruises. I enjoyed rugger very much at school and I was a most enthusiastic tackler of the young monks who indulged us with the occasional game.

At Worth Priory Dom Wulstan-Philipson, an Irish monk and quite deliberately independent of the Headmaster and the Abbot, used to collect a group of us small boys and take them out to readings in a cow shed on the school grounds. This club was known as the Pickwick Club and as well as Dickens we also read a lot of A A Milne and most people in the club assumed names, like Piglet and Pooh. I remember Dom Wulstan-Philipson had the most marvellous reading voice and brought to life for me many exciting literary characters. He ensured that we had a lot of fun in the Pickwick Club as well as learning a few important lessons in life. The most important thing he taught me was you must learn to 'put God before Mammon' and contribute something to the community rather than just devote your life to making money.

Inevitably one had favourites among the monks. One of mine was Dom Maurice Bell at whose ordination I had the honour of carrying the Bishop's crozier. When he saw it was facing the wrong way he whispered, 'You can't carry it that way until you are a bishop'. Dom Maurice Bell was an ex mountain climber and one of our favourite stories about him was the time when one of the boys asked him, 'What would you do if you had a bear behind?', to which he allegedly replied, 'Pull up my skirts and run.'

Dom Maurice Bell later became Headmaster of Worth in 1940 and built the school to 250 boys from 80. At his memorial service the Abbot of Worth said,

'Many monks have, in their particular way, contributed much to Worth's growth and progress, but no single person deserves as great a share of credit for it as Father Maurice. The present good condition of the school, both material and spiritual, is in a very real way a testimonial to him – to his influence St Paul tells us in the second reading this morning (*Romans, 14, 7-12*) how, 'the life and death of each of us has its influence on others'. I have no doubt in my own mind that Father Maurice exerted his influence by his own personal example in the spiritual life. The monastic life mattered for him most in the world, and although he freely

Dom Wulstan-Philipson.

admitted that some aspects of our Benedictine renewal and the changes of the liturgy disturbed him, he accepted those changes with enviable fidelity in the spirit of a truly obedient monk.

'So it was that Father Maurice became a great headmaster, because he was, first and foremost a good monk. He took a personal interest in every boy without ever showing a preference. Those of you who were under him may have been more conscious at the time of awe and respect, but many found afterwards that they could go to him for advice in time of difficulty and would always find an unlimited reservoir of sympathetic and unselfish understanding. It was in this way that he succeeded in winning the lasting respect and affection of a countless number of boys and parents.'

Another favourite was Hubert Van Zeller who wrote a prayer book dedicated to my friend Paddy Higgins called, 'Lord God'. It contained prayers for 'before being beaten' and 'after being beaten'.

At Worth I was given piano lessons by Father Anselm the organist. While he tried valiantly to instill musical talent in me all he managed to do was instill a love of Bach and most lessons consisted of me begging him to play for me. I still remember Father Theodore playing the flute at a concert and receiving encores for Grieg's *Song of Norway*.

I was very happy at Worth Priory but due to a liver upset my parents packed me off to Le Rosey on Lake Geneva to recuperate. The headmaster at Le Rosey was Swiss and his wife was American and very good at looking after us boys. I was placed in a French speaking class for History, Mathematics and Geography, which served to keep me fluent and came in handy at Harrow when I studied Modern Languages. It was also in Switzerland that I discovered a passion for skiing and when the headmaster declared a holiday we all went off joyfully up the Hornberg on skis; in those days there were no lifts. I managed to come third in a junior downhill ski race but due to a touch of bronchitis was unable to complete the second leg.

In 1938 I joined my cousin Shane at Harrow. In my four years there I achieved nothing very spectacular but I very much enjoyed playing racquets as the house Fourth String and played quite a lot of squash as well. On the playing fields I was second row in our rugger team and did quite a lot of cross-country running which was fun, particularly as it invariably ended in a bit of a pub-crawl. But I do remember vividly the day when I won the school steeplechase. I broke a school record but as the stopwatch stopped in the subsequent race I always secretly felt my supposed record was not true. Luckily the course was changed shortly afterwards and therefore my record could not be attacked.

At Harrow I was very lucky to have as my form master, Ronnie Watkins, who used to produce the school play quite brilliantly. We worked very hard for him and we really felt that if we did not get a credit in School Certificate Latin we would be letting him down. As a result we all passed with credit. My recently deceased friend Michael Edwards won French and German prizes in my penultimate year and I won both the following year. We remained good friends despite the competition…

On one occasion I wrote to *The Harrovian* criticising a report on a talk we had been given and consequently got the job for doing the next one. This caused great excitement because the speaker this time was our old family friend Leo Amery on his time in India as the Secretary of State for the Commonwealth. It was an interesting talk and I wrote what I thought was quite a pleasing report.

But surely the greatest excitement of all was when Winston Churchill's Foreign Office Secretary, Jock Colville, brought

Winston down in the war and we sang him our school songs. I remember that we had written a special verse for him and he changed it. It started off, 'Nor less we praise in darker days the leader of our nation' and he said 'Not darker, *sterner* days' and so it has remained, I believe. Jock Colville, an old Harrovian himself, later became secretary to Princess Elizabeth and married one of her ladies in waiting, Lady Margaret Edgerton, a lovely lady with a marvellous sense of humour. I subsequently got to know them both quite well. I remember a skiing holiday with them when Lady Margaret came down to breakfast informing us that, 'Jock's been having royal dreams again'.

I have clear memories of the frosts of 1940 at Harrow when we did a lot of tobogganing in makeshift toboggans down the hill. It was great fun. Also that autumn there was a plentiful supply of conkers and we had a gigantic conker fight, The Grove against Elmfield, neighbouring houses, with knapsacks crammed full of conkers as the only ammunition.

I was no good at cricket at school but enjoyed nothing more than a light-hearted game and so became a member of that well-known team, The Outcasts. One of our favourite matches took place against Dorchester, not least because the village pub was situated conveniently on the green. Our least successful match I remember was against the Wembley Busmen when we never even split the opening part.

At Harrow I also had a lot of fun in the Air Training Corps with the commander Phillip Back and we had an old Napier Lion engine which we painstakingly put together and pulled apart. One day Phillip and I were working on it and somebody from the BBC arrived to ask us to do a talk on the Air Training Corps for the radio. This was my first experience of speaking on the radio and I was amazed when the thing came through that I sounded like a retired Indian Army Colonel. There was great excitement at the time because we got a cheque for about five pounds for our trouble!

When we started learning Turkish, by way of variety a colleague of mine and I decided to publish a magazine which, as we were staying in the house called The Orchard, we named *First Fruits*. One of the best contributions was from my friend Peter Parker.

> What we eat is meat
> But cabbages and spud
> Thud
> With a whine it hits the spine
> Our natural juice
> Its obvious use
> But cannot do it
> Because of the suet
> Which affects a seizure
> A space, then grace
> Thank god for magnesia

I remember very well at mealtimes a diminutive cockney waitress called Connie who would always come round with a jug saying to each of us in her mournful tone, 'Would you like some more gravy?' Which, being young and energetic, we usually did.

Peter and Sandy Wilson did a very brilliant review for us which I said at the time was as good as anything in the West End and sure enough Sandy went on to collaborate with the famous Hermiones, Baddeley and Gingold as well as writing the hit musical, *The Boyfriend*.

SOAS London University

At the end of my career in the Modern Language VI at Harrow I took the scholarship exam for Oxford which unfortunately I failed. However shortly after that I saw an advertisement in *The Times* for students of Modern Languages to study Chinese, Japanese, Turkish and Persian. I thought Turkish sounded a very good idea for after the war and my mother got onto our old friend Leo Amery who thought it was a very good idea too. He himself had been out to Turkey before the 14-18 war reporting for *The Observer*. So some others and I applied for the scholarship (which was for the School of Oriental and African Studies at the University of London) and my friend Gus Ballingal and I were selected to learn Turkish and Sandy Wilson was chosen to learn Japanese.

Navy – Turkey

My naval career started in 1943 with my appointment as the lowest possible form of officer life; namely Probationary Temporary Midshipman, Special Branch, Special Service, Royal Naval Volunteer Reserve.

On signing up the Navy sensibly decided two things. Firstly that we Turkish Scholars had better be sent out to Turkey to improve our knowledge and become first class interpreters, and secondly that they should try and turn us into Naval Officers first. The attempt to turn us into Naval Officers in Portsmouth was most enjoyable and we eagerly absorbed lists of officer-like qualities (OLQs) and absorbed all the naval slang, such as *warming the bell* and *splicing the main brace*.

However the most daunting thing was being put in charge of the rum ration at Portsmouth Barracks where several hundred ratings received their rum every day. It was the responsibility of the Officer in Charge to sign that the rationing had been carried out correctly but faced with three senior Petty Officers with at least fourteen years' service each, one wasn't in any position to query it in the event of a problem!

Rather less daunting a task was an afternoon sailing on the French sailing ship *La Belle Poule* which had escaped from Brest. It was here that we learned the various parts of the boat in English and French and after a cold day's sailing had something I hadn't had before which was rum in tea; a rather satisfactory end to a chilly day.

With that small amount of training we were then shipped out, by way of Liverpool, in a troopship to Suez. The accommodation for the officers aboard the troopship was pretty rudimentary, blocks of thirty-two bunks, four feet high, six feet long and two feet wide, but the ventilation was quite good and even though we twice crossed the Equator it wasn't too uncomfortable.

We arrived in Durban without any incident, stopping to anchor at Capetown for a very short time. In Durban we were right royally entertained and I discovered a very good French restaurant called Chez Marianne in Ploughshare Lane which when I returned forty years later had unfortunately disappeared.

In Durban Gus my bird-watching companion and fellow Harrovian and I took ourselves off to Rob Roy, the Valley of the Thousand Hills, and had a most interesting afternoon wandering through Zulu country looking at the birds; all in the air. The Valley of the Thousand Hills sits in typical African countryside with very little greenery, except thorn bushes and little settlements of Zulus in Rondaval type huts. We stayed in Durban for three weeks. It was very pleasant and the locals only too keen to entertain us with dancing and drinking the local Chateau Brandy.

During the passage from Durban to Suez we young naval officers were given the job of keeping submarine watch from above the bridge. It is not easy to be certain that a shark's dorsal fin is not a submarine's periscope, so it was usually a rather nerve-wracking experience.

The navy was full of potentially nerve-wracking experiences as I found when it was discovered by the officious OC Troops that I kept a diary. Apparently this was a court martial offence but fortunately one of the other officers who knew his King's Regulations and Admiralty Instructions was able to point out that the Midshipman has a duty to keep a journal and the whole matter was dropped.

The passage to Suez was full of little confrontations of this type between the OC Troops and the troops. One of my favourites is the story of the OC Troops and the Australians, who were also taking passage. He had decided that everybody should do PT first thing in the morning. However, the Australians far preferred lying in their hammocks and they organised some voices, a bass and a treble to reply when the infuriated officer came down to find them still in their hammocks. 'What does this mean?', he demanded angrily. And a treble voice replied, 'Shall we tell him?', to which the tenor retorted, 'Tell him what?', and the booming bass answered, 'Tell him to get stuffed'. After that there was no question of the Australians doing PT.

Another time I was Duty Officer on HMS *Nile* when a young medical officer presented himself and asked would I inform SNORSCA that he was on his way. The silly telephonist put me straight to Commodore Young Jameson in the middle of his siesta.

The happiest memories of that passage however are the dances on the quarterdeck. I remember there were two very pretty twin girls Daphne and June on board who were going to join their father, a Cable and Wireless manager in Aden. Their mother was acting as chaperone and I was deputed to go and break down resistance and sure enough we got her agreement for the girls to dance with the naval officers, some of whom kept in touch with them when they got to Alex. I was left with mother!

The landscape on the approach to Suez is characterised by some dingy khaki cliffs. And when we eventually drew near I heard a small Tommy come onto the upper deck and go to the rail and say. 'White Cliffs of Dover – browned off', which clearly expressed his feelings.

In Suez the French Club entertained us with good food (typically steak bearnaise or truite aux manades) before we were sent up to Alexandria to be billeted at the Royal Naval Air Station of El Dikheila. El Dikheila lies on the coastal road between Alexandria and Mersa Matruh, just west of Alexandria. Nearby stand the ruins of an ancient monastery called Enaton. This monastery was built in the fifth century by monks who also left some evidence of their existence in the area of Lake Mariut and Wadi Natrun

On the way to El Dikheila we were treated to a look at the glue factory where everyone's used camel was disposed of and indeed if ever one was to be in any doubt the smell was enough to make its business clear. I was left to bring on the heavy baggage and as a result of the flies of El Dikheila managed to acquire myself a bad case of dysentery. However I struggled on to Cairo with the baggage. My abiding memory of Cairo is certainly the Tutan Khamun exhibition at the museum and seeing four pyramids. Unfortunately in the Officers Club there I was taken severely ill and carted off to the General Hospital so that I arrived in Istanbul three weeks after the rest, travelling alone.

It was quite an interesting journey by rail. We went backwards first to Benha where the line from Port Said branched off from the line from Alexandria and then a troop train took us up to Palestine, stopping about every three hours for food and drink which inevitably consisted of eggs, bacon, sausages and friend bread. On the way I stopped in Haifa where the Naval Mess was looking after a whole lot of Italian officers from the three or four submarines which had surrendered to us. Northern Italians with fair hair and fair beards, they could not have looked less like the typical Italian but were still a very good looking lot. They were very pleasant company and taught me a few useful Italian phrases.

My next stop was at the Tripoli-Syria Naval Base which boasted two officers. I sat myself down and one of them came in and, having completed introductions, he said 'Do you drink?' To which I replied 'Yes, in moderation'.

'Thank God. The other man doesn't', came the weary reply.

On the *Orient Express* from Aleppo to Istanbul I was very lucky to fall in with an American courier who regaled me with various stories of female spies and espionage. I noticed he was very careful to lock his compartment whenever we went for a meal. He used a very neat little gadget, made, I think, of stainless steel, which you put behind the door with the ring sticking through the gap and a large padlock enabled him to leave his less confidential possessions in his compartment.

When I eventually joined my colleagues in Istanbul I found that we had been allocated the Embassy Summer Rest House which was on the Asiatic side of the Bosphorus, near a place called Kadiköy and we were very well looked after with a cook, a housekeeper, gardener and maid. Kadiköy was a typical villa development such as you would find outside other Mediterranean cities. I remember the next-door villa was owned by a man called Djelal Bayar who had the Turkish sugar monopoly and later became Prime Minister. The Turks have a seemingly arbitrary system of income tax; they simply say 'you've been earning a lot recently, I think you should pay now'. In his case I think it was 1,000,000 Turkish lire and somebody must have miscalculated because he still had enough money left to set up his own political party.

You may wonder how we could afford to live this life on the eleven shillings a week Midshipman's wages but fortunately our Cost of Living Allowance was far greater; I think we got about two pounds a day, which more than covered the expenses, so we survived alright. Our occupation was exploring the covered market (the ex-stables of the Sultan) in Istanbul where the fact that we spoke fluent Turkish shook the shop dealers to start with until they got to know us by sight and we tended to collect certain things, particularly what were called *van ishi* (ishi-work); silver cigarette boxes engraved with black lacquer.

There are always things you regret in life. One of my abiding regrets is a particular chess set. I had gone down the Grand Route de Pera in Istanbul to an old antique dealer I knew. It was late in the afternoon and he said 'Why don't we have a game?'. I agreed and he set out the more expensive pieces right in the middle of the shop and proceeded to lose quite convincingly. However at the end of the game I had to admit that I couldn't afford to pay for it so in the end I paid fourteen pounds for a lovely chess set but not like the one I really wanted, which, I think, was about thirty pounds.

We got very fond of our daily breakfast in Istanbul, which consisted of a lovely creamy yogurt and quince marmalade and we made our own drinks for the evening which were very easy because one could buy pure alcohol, mix it with 50% water, put in some lemon and call it vodka.

But perhaps the most exciting thing of all during my time in Istanbul was getting to know Bernard O'Leary. Bernard O'Leary had been the Military Attaché in the days of Ataturk and he was the only man who could play poker all night, drink as much as his host and still remain compos mentis. Now Ataturk thought that the English were effete and by association the Irish too and that really they ought to go into the war on the side of Germany but Bernard O'Leary was the living proof that the English were not effete let alone the Irish. He was extremely good company and I always secretly believed that he was singly responsible for Turkey not coming into the war on the side of Germany.

At any rate Bernard decided that we had to be shown a bit of Istanbul life and held a dinner party for the five of us Turkish Interpreters at Taksims, which had two bars; the top which was known as the Cathedral and the bottom as the Snake Pit. When we got to the Snake Pit Bernard said he knew more about Hungarian dancing girls than any other man alive, which, after seeing him in action, I am more than prepared to believe.

The other great influence on us there was our tutor Ziya Bey, whose correct name in those days was Ziya Fergar because it was customary to invent a surname. Now Ziya Bey was not necessarily a good teacher but such a marvellous source of information. For example he knew what all the different sorts of china were in the Sultan's collection, which at that time was housed at the Dolma Batche. But while I learned a good deal about Famille Rose & Verte from him, the most fascinating thing were his stories of Gallipoli. At Gallipoli he had been General Liman von Sanders' (Commander of the German Forces at Gallipoli) interpreter. Unfortunately as I have said he was not a very good teacher, although we had a lot of fun and I learned how to play backgammon in Turkish, where they still use a lot of Arabic expressions such as *shesh besh*, which is six and five, and *sebai e du*, four and two.

One very exciting interlude in our Turkish duties was the great occasion of our skiing holiday. Our skiing party consisted of my fellow Harrovian Gus, two of the female secretaries from the Embassy, a couple of American Vice Consuls and me. One of the American Vice Consuls, Charlie McVicker (who later went on to become US Ambassador) lived in a flat with the US Consular Shipping Adviser, Hal Noble who, when you rang the doorbell, advanced down the stairway, hand outstretched, no matter who you were, and said 'My, but I'm pleased to see you!' Being older than the rest of us Hal inevitably became known as Uncle Hal.

On this trip we went to Ulu Dagh which is a big mountain, as its Turkish name suggests, just behind Borsa thus we had to go by ship to Borsa with our hired equipment, taking mules from Borsa up to the snow line. When we reached the snow line we were met by tough little porters who carried all our baggage up to the hotel, which was quite some way above. The skiing was lots of fun but not particularly sophisticated because there were no pistes and no lifts. I unfortunately went down with bronchitis but there was a very nice German doctor in the hotel who insisted on my taking some antibiotic BASF tablets which in due course cured it. When the time came to leave the others went down first leaving me in the company of a man they couldn't stand, who later turned out from his card to be the Romanian Vice-Consul, rejoicing in the name of Count Constantine Von Berispec. When it became time to go down we both asked for a hotel room at the same time and were told there was only one left which we could share. I said 'Yes' quickly and we did. We went on to have the most marvellous Turkish bath in a genuine and very ancient *hammam*, one of the finest in Turkey with ceramics out of this world, followed by a most enjoyable dinner together, not least because this chap knew everybody in the hotel, largely consisting of exiled opposition political figures. Before I left the hotel my new companion handed me a bundle of letters which he asked me to post in Istanbul. With hindsight I dare say this incident was probably one of the reasons he was subsequently thrown in jail for espionage…

Our favourite bar in Istanbul was 'Elli's'. Elli served the best dry martini in town. The Assistant Naval Attaché had censored my letters and told me 'You are not to go to Elli's Bar, she's an enemy alien'. To which I replied 'Sorry sir, I gather that her third husband was Dutch'. However on my next visit whom did I see but the Assistant Naval Attaché himself. We ignored each other and no more was ever mentioned.

The best teas in town were to be had at a Hungarian cake shop. I remember a party of Germans speaking English so we all spoke German. A lot of intelligence business was carried on in such teashops and we used to studiously ignore anyone we knew to be talking to a contact.

The La Fontaines and Whittals (one of the best-known business families of English origin in Istanbul) asked all of us to their house for New Year 1945. The eldest La Fontaine boasted that he had a very great way of keeping sober; by taking a large spoonful of olive oil before drinking. Unfortunately on New Year's Eve he was out cold before midnight so we didn't try his solution. In Turkey we used to make our own vodka using 100% alcohol. A friend in academic circles checked that it was in fact just that with only 3% water. The wicked man used to make a drink with 50% banana liqueur, which tasted rather sweet and innocuous but was guaranteed to get any one of his girlfriends swiftly drunk.

I have mentioned before my passion for bird-watching but in Turkey we had to be a little bit more careful because when we were out in the hills we quite often used to get inadvertently involved with Turkish Army Platoon manoeuvres. Probably not such a good idea. However we were lucky enough never to get rounded up. We also bought a boat which we re-rigged and used for fishing and we were taught how to use what Turkish fishermen call a *chapari* which has between sixteen and thirty-two hooks on it and on occasions enables one to catch a full house of mackerel. It was typical of the Turkish character that when we applied for an official Fishing Licence were told in a manner combining hospitality and bureaucracy that, 'Fishing licences are not allowed for foreigners during wartime and it would be very expensive for you to get a licence but you can fish all the same', which we did with great success.

On one fishing expedition we sailed past a large place on (the point) with anti-aircraft guns bearing a large notice in Turkish saying '*Dangerous and Forbidden Military Area*'. Well, a little later after our trip it had been arranged for all the bigwigs to watch a searchlight display. The only trouble was that the first night they came the searchlight wouldn't turn on, so they had it all to pieces and put it together and then the next night it still wouldn't work. Just more proof to us that the Turks are very hard-working but not necessarily very brilliant engineers.

I had got to know the secretaries at the Embassy fairly well by this stage, particularly those in the Military Attaché's department. Catherine Kyffen was a very keen sailor and Margot Firebrace whose uncle, Commander Firebrace, rather appropriately commanded wartime fire brigades. One Saturday morning in early 1945 we got a message that we were to give the staff time off because three gentlemen were arriving. One was Nicky Elliott, the Assistant Military Attaché in charge of Intelligence and son of Claude Aurelius, the Eton Headmaster. The other was a gentleman who I assumed was the Head of the CIA owing to his accent, and the third I deduced was a German speaker (evident from the phrase 'Were you once in Switzerland?', which is a direct translation of the equivalent German word order). The German visitor was extremely helpful in giving me the name of a much better hairdresser in Istanbul and was a very pleasant and affable gentleman. At one stage during the visit I was asked to go to the station to buy a ticket for Aleppo. Whilst out I happened to catch sight of a Turkish newspaper, which by that time I could read fluently, reporting that Herr Willi Hamburger, 3rd Secretary of the German Legation, had disappeared. I suddenly had no doubt as to whom our third guest was.

The next time I saw Margot Firebrace I said that we had had Willi staying for the weekend to which she replied, 'I wondered where he'd been'. She had an item of expenses 'parasol for lady to hide behind' and she recounted how a message had got through that he was at the Londra Hotel and could he be taken from there. The Londra Hotel is very close to the British Embassy and he had asked to be picked up after breakfast. In fact in a subsequent discussion with Nicky Elliott at lunch one day I told him of my side of the Willi story, and Nicky informed me that it wasn't breakfast at all it was dinner. Apparently they had shot out through this kitchen and the only place to go was the British Embassy, and that's where Willi spent the night before coming on to us.

I think it was after this that we were invited to have a drink at the Embassy with the Ambassador, Sir Hugh Knatchbull Hugison, who had as his valet the iniquitous Cicero. A very good film was subsequently made, based on the photocopying of the contents of the Ambassador's safe and the contents being sold to the German Embassy. Ironically the German Chancellery refused to believe that the papers were not planted to be found, despite Ambassador Von Papen's belief that they were genuine.

It was a curious tradition at the British Embassy that one should have as one's servants Albanians because they hated the Turks and were therefore assumed to be loyal to the British. The falsity of this assumption was all too often demonstrated. My parting memory of Turkey, and again testament to the sterling character of the Turkish people, was when we were leaving and Ziya Bey informed us that his son-in-law was Chief Customs Officer and would we please pack anything we were taking out of the country down the sides of our cases. We obeyed and we went into the Chief Customs Officer's office where we were offered coffee and cigarettes and he duly searched our cases, deliberately not looking down the sides. As friends of this family this was a free service but had we been other than that the Embassy staff would have told us how much we had to give. He was then receiving less salary than I was as a Midshipman so obviously was expected to recoup from his position.

Ziya Bey told me a nice story about a *pasha* whose son fell into the Bosphorus and was rescued. The rescuer's father later asked for a job for his son and the *pasha* said 'Right he can be my Chief Collector of Taxes'. Unfortunately he did everything beautifully, kept exact records of everything that was owed and was collected and at the end of the year was fired. Of course the *pasha* was approached by the young man's father who was desperate and said 'But my son has done so well'. To which the *pasha* replied, 'Don't tell me. If the man cannot make enough money to retire after one year as my Chief Collector of Taxes he's incompetent'.

When I left Turkey I was a first class Turkish interpreter attached to Eastern Mediterranean Coastal Forces. On the way down I had a week's leave at the Naval Rest Camp at Ali, a lovely villa in the hills above Beirut, which I always thought would have been marvellous in skiing weather.

In April 1944 I joined Bill Toombs, the RNVR Lt Cdr in charge and the two other subs on the advance CFB as the new Intelligence Officer and resident Turkish interpreter. We three subs shared all duties. With Navy House and its 30 ratings across the harbour under the eye of the experienced chief, these were not heavy. Our life was anaesthetised with copious quantities of gin consumed at noon and night, rations being drawn from no less than four NAAFIs.

Visitors were frequent. Most popular were Jock Lapraik, proud of the £10,000 price on his head; Andy Lassen, eager to increase his tally of aircraft and dead members of the wretched 999th Fortress Battalion and George Jellicoe in his HSL, disguised as an 8 knot pleasure cruiser. Most unpopular were parties of brigadiers on picnic, who justified their visit by devising a novel defence plan for our island which they expected to see attacked from Rhodes. The culmination was a scheme whereby the defending force had to climb to the top of the mountain after dark and return again before dawn, guaranteeing surprise (not least to our unfortunate Indian OC troops).

At Navy House we slept comfortably guarded by one sentry. Doc McLean was allowed down to sample our whisky. One evening, descending the steps from our beautiful Italianate building he turned left where the pretty rail ended and crashed four feet to the quay. As I reached him I received his diagnosis, 'A compos fracture of the radial: the man that built those steps must have been a Campbell!'. The Indian army doctor was summoned and Doc Mclean insisted on an ether mask which proved ineffective after all that whisky, so we had to hold him down while his vilified colleague in fact did a perfect job.

Between the hills was a gap known as 'Bomb Alley'. On the point was an old *breda* left by the Italians, recently repainted by a rating bored with naval grey who had found pots of red and green; it would have stood a good chance of winning at an agricultural show. In the event of an attack the first one there was allowed to fire it. The only time I won I was lucky to miss an idiotic Hudson who had chosen this foolhardy route from Rhodes.

Fuelling caiques (this is a work horse of the Eastern Mediterranean. Anything from small fishing boat to large coaster) with a few cans of diesel was no problem but an ELCO from Alex, even at 18 knots needed 1600 gallons (400 cans) which had to be manhandled from the camouflaged fuel depot. Not a popular visitor, unlike Martin Solomon who unloaded a generous quantity of liberated Santorin wine. Or even the captive Germans from Symi who, locked in the mosque, were persuaded to sing Lili Marlene while their women cooked our dinner (a pleasant change from my ten varieties of corned beef).

It was the shortage of fresh meat (and not the charms of the lighthouse keeper's daughter) that led to a combined operation to the otherwise deserted nearby island whose goat population had run wild. Every conceivable weapon (grenades excepted) was used. I was most disappointed at my lack of success, spraying the rocks liberally with a Thompson sub-machine gun. We eventually bagged just two goats between us. Greater success however was achieved fishing. My own record was 70 three quarter pounders with one Mills grenade, thanks to the simultaneous arrival of two shoals in the little pool near the point. The crew of our Greek tender, which proudly bore the name *Phut Phut*, was even more successful using one and a quarter pound charges.

Intelligence duties were light. In my charge was a Top Secret book entitled *Bases and Anchorages on the SW Coast of Turkey* to which I was very occasionally able to add some report. A Cypriot rating interpreted for escaping Greek fishermen and when my questions elicited a flood of Greek from a fisherman, the interpreter would say 'He says yes'. No wonder I was forced to learn Greek as well. But nothing was as evocative as the Deerstalker's Report from Rhodes in which I fondly imagined a swarthy Greek with a with a spyglass and deerstalker hat.

An official visit to the local Turkish governor by OC troops and NOIO (Naval Officer in Charge) required my services as interpreter. All went well until Bill decided to explain the system of social insurance planned for post-war New Zealand…

Shortly after this, one of our supply caiques sank itself. LCT13 was despatched to raise her with the help of Turkish divers. Good manners dictated that I share their food. But the resultant dysentery sent me to share Doc Davidson's accommodation in the cathedral charnel house. With a temperature of 105° I saw the town burn down like something from *Dante's Inferno*. Thank God for the Doc, sulpha guanide and on this occasion an ELCO to evacuate me (physically not medically).

Back in Alex, having recovered from dysentery, I returned to the Coastal Force base. During the journey back there I asked the black South African driver who collected me how he liked Egypt. To which he replied, 'Alright sah, but I can't stand these wogs'.

On my arrival I was informed of Operation Haddock, the ad hoc plan (which well warranted its name) for clearing the minefields and entering Pireaus. Because of our experience in Khios, where we encountered several nasties, it was decided that we should check Pireaus very thoroughly with me taking all the dinghies of the flotilla. I devised a system of non-magnetic markers, paving stone sinkers and corks to float. We had to have a practice for the dinghies to proceed in line abreast and this took place in Aboukir Bay, the scene of Nelson's Battle of the Nile.

Greece

WE SAILED FOR Greece at 0100 on Friday 13th September 1945, to everyone's fury. Why not 2300 on 12th? We arrived at our starting point (clear of Cape Turlo), having sailed round in a square suffering the most uncomfortable 'beam seas'.

The flotilla of inshore sweepers carried two officers, but as the third officer I was given the choice of joining the latest recruit or my rather drunken South African friend Ken Wiley. I took what proved to be a fortunate choice. Contact mines which had been cut were usually sunk by rifle fire but on this occasion the flotilla leader caught a mine which didn't cut and the new recruit ran into it, killing all those on the bridge. One of my command had been sunk and my first thought was not that I might have been there but , 'Oh dear, it was a brand new dinghy'. The whole operation was disastrous. The inshores were not given time to clear the contact mines and two fleet sweepers, Larne and Clinton, were badly damaged. That evening we performed a magnetic sweep of the inner harbour and went alongside. As spare officer I was able to stretch my legs, but my walk was interrupted by a small boy in a sailor's suit who was pushed through the barbed wire with a large bouquet of flowers. I took them, patted the boy on the head and rushed back to the safety of my ship. Needless to say, Ken blamed my flowers for his hangover the next day.

After that I was placed in the operations room at the naval academy but as there wasn't room for me on the HQ yacht, I was

Laura Pandos with Dermot.

made to stay in the Grande Bretagne Hotel in Athens. One evening Frank Ramsier, who was SOO (Staff of Operations) was going to a party and said to me, 'Dermot, sail CS15 to arrive at Khios at first light'. This was the first and last time I have issued orders to an admiral. CS15 commanded a squadron hoisting its flag in Ajax, so with all the authority of an SBNO (Senior British Naval Officer), I ordered Admiral Mansfield to sail at a certain time via various swept channels.

Jock Campbell had a bad habit of shooting off signals last thing

Laura Pandos.

at night and it was rumoured that those in his command tended to ignore any with a time of origin after 22.00. On one occasion he sent me to do a report on the port of Kavala. The only problem was that the bridge of the Struma River was down and travelling with Harold Caccia of the Foreign Office we had to use a makeshift ferry running on a tight wire across the river. They had just tipped one vehicle into the river when I took charge of this combined operation and we managed to cross safely.

Kavala was a fantastically good port and at the time, as now, the main exporter of Greek tobacco. Moreover the army had fixed a very good rate of return for the Bulgarian leva so we managed to live quite well. Historically known as Neapolis, Christoupolis and Eaiala, Kavala has been inhabited since Neolithic times and as well as the breathtaking view of the island of Thasos across the Aegean, the city boasts a 5th century castle, last rebuilt during the time of the Turkish occupation.

Our return to Salonika (Greek Thessaloniki) passed fairly uneventfully and we got back to Athens in one piece. The next day there was a political demonstration through which our taxi drove to the Grande Bretagne Hotel. I had barely got to the first floor when I heard shots from the police station on the corner. There were shots from the crowd and a number of casualties. This was the start of the revolution which would last until March 1949 when the Communist forces were defeated.

Prior to this Jock had asked me to be his representative at General Scobie's 3 corps headquarters and had introduced me to Brigadiers G and Q (Operations and Supply) and I was summonsed to attend their conferences at 9.00 and 16.00 where I was asked the range of Ajax's guns and thanks to Jock's forethought I was able to use the naval telegraphists on the roof to get a reply (which was approximately 20,000 yards). The revolution was in full swing when I got a call from a very frightened Jock to the effect that I was to tell General Scobie that his interpreter had just been shot dead beside him. This I phoned to the General's PA and thereafter anyone who had to pass the Fix Brewery on the Phaleron road took an armoured vehicle. All, that is, except for a colleague of mine, Archie Yuill who took a bullet across the top of his fingers and might well have been killed.

Admiral Turle (nicknamed 'the Boy Scout') drove to Piraeus in his official car, telling ELAS (the communist resistance organisation) that he *must* get through because he was responsible for bringing food into Greece. He was sent back in an armoured car. Next day a Sherman tank forced ELAS to evacuate their building (which was at right angles to the palace). The military told me that it was safe to go to the Admiral's house but he was advised to move into our building, so I went round to find him protected by very frightened marines who saw him across to our Tamion building where he had a table and chair in our corridor. Unfortunately ELAS had some Italian 75s which were firing into our side of the building. The US naval attaché was visiting us when we both had to dive under my desk as a shell hit the office below.

My next memory is of Christmas Day when Winston paid a flying visit and I missed my Christmas lunch! Apparently meeting with Archbishop Damaskinos aboard Ajax the latter was thought to be one of the jokers dressed up and was thoroughly mobbed. My old friend Aleko Matsas was deputed by his foreign office to show Winston round the Parthenon. Winston loved being under fire but Aleko was not amused and I got a most entertaining description of the visit from him.

I will never forget New Year's Eve in the Grande Bretagne when we all gathered for drinks by candlelight. ELAS had taken over the nearby Marathon dam, our source of electricity, and we all sat on the floor. I was next to the Russian representative, Colonel Popoff, who gave his glass for a refill, sank it and said, 'Vermouth, no good. Give me an ouzo'.

The Chief of Staff's staff moved from the Grande Bretagne into the Skouze House before General Plastiras could take it. I remember the Sunday when, in full No10 whites, I was walking to church and a shell went over and hit the Bulgarian Legation on the other side of the road, confirming for me that you don't hear the shell that hits you. This one was not fused and did not explode and I walked on, my lovely whites unsullied by throwing myself flat. For which I was duly grateful.

There was a nasty incident when the ML, stationed to stop vehicles on the Eleusis Road fired on an American ambulance. I knew Ken Lloyd's gun crew very well. He had chosen the four dimmest men in his crew, knowing they would not be frightened by fire and being told to shoot anything that came along the road. They did not obviously think that ambulances would be the exception. I had some difficulty explaining this to an irate American Brigadier whose colleague had lost a man killed by an Italian shell in the car park. My sympathy was lessened by the fact that the Americans were neutral, accusing us of trying to put in a royalist government. In fact we had landed Papandreou right beside the one danger I had spotted; a sunken ammunition barge with butterfly bombs.

Before the troubles I had met two charming Greek girls, Laura Pandos and Irene Lambros. Laura's family provided me with a home from home and subsequently taught me a lot about Greece. Her mother was a Benaki of the famous museum family. I always called her mother, '*tante*' and we often spoke French together. Her father was something of a boulvardier and we called him, 'the old man'. Sadly Irene and Laura are both now dead but Irene's son, Laura's godson still keeps in touch and in fact Laura was godmother to my second son.

When the troubles were over we used to charter a boat at weekends and a party of twenty or more with two guitarists would go to some nearby port where there was accommodation. I made friends with Kutzi Baltadzi who sang on Athens radio and who taught me many Greek songs (which I still remember now). I also remember a dance we gave at the Chief of Staff's mess, where Laura got me waltzing, like my mother had taught me from her days in Austria.

After the troubles I was appointed Naval Liaison Officer Kavala. They wanted a more junior officer because the RNVR

2½ did not get on with Captain Papodopoulos who was in command.

I had a very happy further three months in Kavala. The most traumatic incident being only when I lost the key of my confidential book safe, which I needed for routing merchant ships. Captain Papadopoulos arranged for the local locksmith to open it the next morning, which he did with consummate ease. When I arrived in Kavala I told Petty Officer Baldwin, an ex-submariner, to be responsible for the discipline at Navy House. I did not want any defaulters. The only problem we really ever had was that two of the lads were shacked up with local girls who had to get away when we left and I agreed to lend the men our 30cwt for that purpose.

We used to take the lorry to explore Xanthe where the local wine was so foul that even the iron-stomached ratings couldn't drink it. On Sundays I used to borrow the Greek NOIC boat and with some from the local aid agencies would sail across to the island of Thasos, famous in antiquity for its bees. I remember a party at which no one spoke less than three languages and we had no single language between us. Just to add to the variety, our hosts were Dutch.

When my friend Martin Solomon went north with Andy Lassen he threw me the keys of his jeep which I used to take a party to Delphi. When he eventually got the keys back he told me a story of how he was driving their jeep along a side road at Voros when they met a Tiger tank coming the other way. They disappeared but later found the jeep parked outside the tavern with the keys still in it. So they leapt in and quickly drove away. Martin told me that Andy said, 'It was well you got the jeep back otherwise I would have killed you'. Martin was convinced he would have done as well!

The next jeep I had enabled me to visit Delphi again and on

one magical day to drive beyond Marathon to a little tavern on the beach, accompanied by two officers of Force 133 from the Evangelistera. The fishermen were just pulling in their nets so we chose our own fish for lunch, preceded by a delicious omelette and washed down with a slightly sparkling retsina, as good as champagne any day.

My next visit to Greece was with M9/19, the escape organisation. I was offered Rome or Athens but as I knew Greece better I opted for the latter. In Greece we called ourselves the Allied Screening Commission and our job was to make files on the stories of everybody who had helped Allied and military personnel to escape the Germans or had taken part in active resistance. One of the major problems we encountered was that people like the Cypriots were hard to uncover and could join families working for them and possibly marry a daughter. The rewards we gave them went from £5 General Unspecified Assistance (GUA) to pensions for widows. However, what was more highly prized was a certificate signed by Field Marshal Alexander, which we gave out sparingly.

When I arrived in Greece I discovered that one of the existing team had already secured the organisation's yacht and was off the West Coast. It was therefore proposed that I charter a *caique* and do the East Coast. The advice from the Sea Transport Officer was to choose one which carried a cargo which shouldn't get wet, such as grain or cement. We found an appropriate vessel, a skipper, his son and an experienced engineer. Like all Greek engineers he was brilliant at making repairs using bits of cigarette tins or toothpaste tubes. Apart from the crew I had a British Captain in the artillery and a Greek 2nd Lieutenant as interpreter. What better way to spend the summer than sailing down the East Coast of Greece; Aiyina, Póros, Idhra, Leonidhion.

Typically one would meet the *papas*, who knew what his

congregation had been up to and regaled one with sticky preserves. On one occasion we came to a threshing floor looking centuries old and we were greeted by a Greek who had probably never even been to Athens and who said, 'Hiya Johnny, I was in Chicago'.

In Idhra we had rather a lot of fun when we discovered that a whole load of Australians who had been hidden in a convent. It must have been rather a pleasant change for the nuns…

I had an unfortunate experience at one of the mess parties when the Naval 30cwt which I had been using to transfer guests in front of the offices disappeared. I had left the vehicle with strict instructions to the colonel's driver to keep an eye on it but when I came down, both had gone. Police reports ran that it had knocked over a fruit barrel on its way out of Athens. We knew it would never be found and would probably be cannibalized for spare parts. I was clearly most to blame and Admiral Arthur George Talbot devised a punishment to fit the crime by making me SBNOG's Transport Officer. There was an advantage however, in that I wrote my own driving licence without ever having had a test. In Athens, I gave the tests.

It was on my second visit to Greece that Monty (Field Marshal Montgomery) came to visit. The event was supposed to be Army Officers only, except for an Airforce Harrovian, Ramsay who had been head of the school. Monty held the stage in the theatre, telling stories against himself.

'When I was a young man, they said to succeed in the army you had to be a bit of a cad. Well I am a bit of a cad'.

He also told the story of when he fought in the 1914-18 war and had to exchange his sword for a pistol because it was an encumbrance.

My return home was as Spare Watchkeeping Officer aboard a Hunt Class destroyer. We arrived in Malta the day after the hottest day they had ever had (35°). I remember the engine room of a friend's LCI reaching a temperature of 58° and being unfit for sailing but I have always loved the feeling of the heat getting through to my bones. With all my cousins in Malta it was very sad that we had to sail after twenty-four hours but we stopped in Gibraltar, picking up silk stockings and fresh fruit.

All in all it was quite a nostalgic homecoming. In the words of the song, 'the first land we sighted, it was the Dodman'. And as Rame Head came into view the green of England was one of the most pleasant surprises of my life.

Business

Having set 65 as a good retirement age for directors, I have now been retired for over 13 years. My father went on as Deputy Chairman of an insurance company until aged 80 but he said he regarded the last 5 years in lieu of a pension. I can't pretend that anyone would be interested in a litany of the posts I have filled nor could I remember the dates, but with the benefit of hindsight I can look at some of the high points of my career and the various roles I have adopted.

I said earlier that one of the attractions of going into business is the power and that is power to do the things one wants to see done. When I wrote terms of reference for my position as chairman of Calor Gas, first on the list was to remove the Chief Executive if he wasn't adequate and then find a suitable replacement. I was very fortunate in my choices at Calor Gas, Low and Bonar and Brentford Electric. One of the sadnesses of my career is that when I made one of these necessary changes at Hugh Smith I incurred the enmity of the Chief Executive's wife whom I considered an admirable woman, but these are the sacrifices one often has to make in business. I'm not sure whether I put it second on my list of Chairman's duties but I always considered it my duty to bring out at the board table the talents of the various Members of the Board so that they were all allowed and encouraged to make a contribution.

Having been introduced to Warburgs, the merchant bank, who courted me because of my IC Gas position, I was invited to represent them on the bank board of the newly formed Parisbas Limited. I said at the time that I would probably learn more from them than they learned from me and this turned out to be true. In fact they lost so much money on foreign exchange dealing that they had to close it down and make it a branch. I had been warned of this danger and knew a first class foreign exchange dealer, Rudi Weissweiler, who had worked with Helmut Schröder and I recommended that they bring him onto the Board, which is what he wanted. However they refused and lost a mint of money and I secretly couldn't help but feel it served them right. Helmut Schröder's dictum was 'All I ask of my foreign exchange dealers is that they shouldn't lose money'. In that game if you make money you make a lot and vice-versa.

I have great memories of Jean Reyre whose presence on the Parisbas Board was a great joy to all of us. He was a first class brain who one might have thought of as the personification of that media bogey, a Gnome of Zurich. Ralph Jarvis who was Chairman at the time used to say 'There are only two things wrong with this Board, one is Reyre's dark glasses and the other is Dermot's slide rule'. Having been trained as a consultant I liked to check figures provided to the board with my slide rule and very frequently found errors in the percentages. While a hand-held calculator would have been better still a slide rule was still then the engineer's weapon. We all believed the rumour that when Reyre's mistress committed suicide he wore a black tie in public for many weeks. Ralph Jarvis eventually died because his wife, as a Christian Scientist, did not approve of normal medical advice.

At this time I was also representing the Association of Catholic Managers and Employers on the National Committee of the Lay Apostolate of which I was Chairman and which was subsequently developed into the National Association of Business Ethics and whose meetings I continue to attend with great interest. I have always argued that ethical business is good business although I am aware that there is considerable temptation for big companies to breach the rules, but, as my daughter says, 'You will only ever do this successfully in the short term.'

At the National Committee I got elected to the chair, as often happened, and my most interesting experience was going to Rome and chairing a plenary session in four languages, of which the three predominant ones were French, German and English and I found myself doing translations between all three, which at that time I could still do with some ease. Italian was an official language but close enough to Latin for one normally to get by. The National Committee provided an interesting eye-opener for me to the problems of the Third World and I remember Africans telling me that in a developing country they could not afford Western democracy where you had your best men spread between rival parties. They needed a unitary government with all the best brains roped in more along American lines.

I would have to say that the most enjoyable part of my business career overall was my relationship with the Chief Executive of Petrofina, Adolph Demeure. He had rooms by his heated swimming pool below his miniature chateau south of Brussels where my wife and I often used to stay the weekend. He had planted the spacious grounds with rhododendrons and azaleas and on a Sunday morning he and I would walk down to the village church and pick up hot croissants on the way back. On Monday morning we would leave in his little baby Renault, setting a good example on fuel conservation. There I would read papers until the executive meeting at nine o'clock, which was useful in getting to know all the chief executives in the group. Basically Demeure made all the decisions but if there were some question of lesser importance he would often take a vote so that the appearance of democracy was preserved.

One evening we went for a walk in the wood and gathered mushrooms but we eventually decided not to eat them because Adolphe said he wouldn't want the gardener to arrive in the room 'like Fortinbras in Hamlet and see a mass of corpses.'

Demeure often had dinner parties at the house, a miniature French château with lovely panelling found in various places around the world. The dinner parties at the chateau often produced a host of interesting characters and I spent many happy times there: we even kept our own gun boots.

After Leon Lambert I was the most senior director and represented a considerable stake of IC Gas but Adolphe said that the introduction of an executive committee would take place over his dead body, which it in fact was, so after his death we had a Directors' Executive Committee (Comité de Direction) on which I served. The main political issue at that time was with our Finnish colleagues to build a new ethylene cracker in Antwerp whence a pipeline went down to our polypropylene plant.

Commenting on the Belgian situation, I remember Adolphe saying that it was sad that there was just three parties; Flanders, Wallonia and Brussels and if there had been seven they could have had more of a federal approach to their problems. While I never learned to speak Flemish properly I made a point of greeting the workmen round the Antwerp refinery in their own language. At that time I was making almost weekly visits to Brussels. I also had a good friend in the distribution side Pierre de Tilesse who enjoyed partridge shooting and on a couple of occasions I joined him. The pheasant shooting in Belgium was rather different to ours because the idea was to surround the wood and have beaters come in from all sides and flush everything out to the surrounding guns. It was also interesting that at the end of the season they did not go in for our policy of shooting cocks only because they felt if too many cocks were killed the hens would stray.

It was during my period as Director of Petrofina that I joined the Banque Belge in London, an arm of the Societé Generále which also controlled Traction et Electricité with a large slice like us of Petrofina. The joy of serving on the Banque Belge board was that, thanks to Paddy O'Brien, I got to know something about banking and benefited from prime experience of the art from Lord O'Brien, a former Governor of the Bank of England who had been put in to stiffen up the board. I vividly remember celebrating his 75th birthday with one of the best wines in the Societé Generále's cellars, namely an Haut Brion (which, interestingly, is a corruption of the Irish O'Brien).

I was partly responsible for getting two other IC Gas Directors onto the board, Sir Peter Hope and Sir Philip de Zlueta. Phillip was on the Board of Tanganyika Concessions and had other business related reasons too for visiting Brussels. When our chairman fell ill I was also able to get the well-deserved promotion of Fernand Rombouts to the position of Chairman and Chief Executive of the Antwerp Gas Company. I spent many good evenings in the company of Fernand and his colleagues. Fernand was short with dyed red hair, hardly covering his bald pate. He was fantastic company and very popular with our clients.

At Electrogas I was a Deputy Chairman and therefore given priority treatment in touring our nuclear energy production. I was sometimes appalled at the somewhat light-hearted approach to accidents. One day we had a leak of contaminated iodine gas one day and the engineer said 'We needn't fear for the cows and milk because any cow affected would have been swimming in the middle of the River Skelt'. This I didn't think funny.

We also had an interesting chemical plant which produced a

range of carbon products and coke ovens which provided the raw material for gas. The Belgians refer to towns gas as *gas fatale*, which means it is a by-product of charcoal-carbons you can't help producing and not to the fact that if you inhale it is fatal. Nevertheless an appropriate designation.

Another great pleasure I have derived from my directorships apart from visits to Belgium, was the time I spent in Africa. The directors always said that nobody went on safari except under Low and Bonar canvas and it's true we owned the West African Canvas Company, the Central African Canvas Company, the East African Canvas Company and the South African Canvas Company, all of whose operations I visited often with Jack Stewart-Clark a Euro MP whom I got onto our Board with the assistance of head-hunters. Jack I could depend on to have the right management view on any question, but sadly after we left the Board allowed our Chief Executive to be tempted away and the company has gone steadily down in the market, which emphasises my point that you cannot pay too much for the right Chief Executive.

At Lagos Airport we had somebody to meet visitors off the plane and to see them through customs. This was a great help. The roads in to town were by now so bad that many firms had a boat and went that way from their houses to the office. When we got to the manager's house we found the same arrangement. Our Lagos board was quite influential and included the head of the Hausa Community in Lagos. I have graphic memories of my later visit to Khano. The first man to get out of the plane was the local ruler and a band of others had come to meet him at the steps of the aircraft but unfortunately a bus was coming for the rest of us and the driver, with his eye fixed on the celebrations, ran straight into the wing of an aircraft which no doubt wrote off both the bus and the aircraft.

It was on the same visit that my friend, Hilary Ihueze, who was a local chief south of Owerri, arranged a party for me in his new house. Champagne of different makes and different vintages and palm wine were assembled, mats were put down on the roof under the stars and the babies laid upon these while their mothers could go dancing in the yard. There was a giant xylophone made from huge tree trunks which acted as a bass and the music was fascinating. There is a local habit, a form of excuse me, whereby the woman comes along with a ten *nirai* note and slaps it on the head of the man with whom she wants to dance.

I remember Hilary being asked where he stood in the family, saying he was the eldest of sixteen. His father had had three wives and I found myself dancing with the third widow. Although the combination of palm wine and champagne was certainly dangerous, I didn't suffer any ill-effects.

In Central Africa we had a Director who had his own private menagerie. Most guests did a double take as they came round the corner of a corridor to meet a stuffed crocodile. His two lions had mauled him and his wife successively but everybody seemed to have recovered. His ridgeback hounds used to chase the baboons and often got worsted in the process. The Director had a tame cheetah and there is a photograph of me holding her in my arms. They are the most beautiful animals to watch. Cheetahs are the most beautiful example of efficient design and they are the animals with the highest acceleration, which also makes them among the best hunters.

This director also had a plane and he and his wife used to fly from Ndola to Lusaka where we had some plastic manufacture and an office base. On one occasion we went to Lusaka to see the President Kenneth Kaunda to present him with a cheque from our company for wildlife preservation.

I backed IC Gas's acquisition of CompAir because, with

nationalisation there were few power companies for sale. It was also a leader in its field of compressed air, able to beat continental competition. By installing the latest machine tools we were able to offset the disadvantages of location in Cornwall. But my group chairman received an offer for, CompAir from another chairman, which I could not promise to match. I said that I considered our actions bad for the company, its employees and the country but good for shareholders, so I could not oppose it. A sad day.

I wrote the following words on their demise…

> Friends, colleagues, countrymen, lend me your ears
> I come to bury CompAir not to praise it.
> The evil that firms do lives after them
> The good is oft interred with their boards
> So let it be with CompAir. The noble Stephens
> Hath thought that CompAir was mismanaged
> If it were so, it were a grievous fault
> And grievously hath CompAir answered it
> Here under leave of Freddie and the rest
> Come I to speak at CompAir's obsequies.
> It was our pride, happy were we to serve
> But Stephens is an honourable man.
> We have brought many orders home to Slough
> Whose profits did the general coffers fill
> Did this in CompAir seem mismanagement?
> Yet Stephens thinks we were mismanaged
> And Stephens is an honourable man.
> You all do know that our head office
> Would soon have yielded cash for our concern
> Some other asset too – was this mismanagement
> Yet Stephens thinks we were mismanaged
> And Stephens is an honourable man.
> O Judgement, thou are fled to brutish beasts
> And men have lost their reason. Bear with me

> My heart is now in grief for Comp Air
> And I must pause – and give you all a toast
>
> TO COMPAIR – WHAT MIGHT HAVE BEEN

I very much enjoyed my time on the so-called Cadbury Committee, particularly as we met in the Bank of the England under the portrait of Montague Norman. My main contribution was to avoid recommending too much power for shareholders on specific matters. For example, I said that it was not practical for a committee to decide what an Executive Director should earn. The Board had to decide based on market conditions

One of the other sides of having the power to see what you want done is seeing that justice is a conscious aim of management at all levels. The most painful management task is always the dismissal of staff but there are many ways of softening the blow. I have always found that taking the blame for making an unsuitable promotion and suggesting alternative lines in which their abilities would be better used. I remember telling a man that he would never be worth £10,000 a year as a Chief Executive but that he was already worth that as a sales director.

All in all it is rather fun being Chairman. Once you are sure you've got the right Chief Executive you can relax and watch that he does not get over-ambitious as many seem to of late. I am very conscious of the fact that recommendations can only be implemented with the support of line management. The consultant needs to consider who he is going to use as the innovator and it is often best if you can persuade the individual that it was his/her idea in the first place. In so many cases one is fighting the argument, 'this is the way we've always done it' and the major obstacle is persuading people that there is room for change and that the change will be a positive thing.

During my business career I spent several years on the boards of investment trusts in Scotland and as a consequence I am a strong advocate of using trusts as the best way to achieving a spread of risk. The Scots seem to avoid the Gadarene Swine Syndrome that can be so destructive to the City and IT market. The London Stock Market follows fashion, which leads the price of shares to rise. The Scots say no and avoid the rush, be it automation or information technology. They are by nature cautious and rightly give home to many investment trusts.

Over almost any long period the benefit of equities as opposed to gilt-edged is clear. Nevertheless a substantial holding of gilts is a further precaution I would advise, as this can be easily liquidated in the event of buying a house or needing capital for a business venture.

In my own career I have found property to be a most beneficial investment and I have known liquidations where the rise in the value of land and buildings has fully reimbursed shareholders in a liquidation

Although personally I have done well from investing in my own companies, I do not encourage my employees to invest savings in their own firm, however attractive the terms. Most people's job represents a major investment of time and skill, to lose this and your savings at the same time is an unnecessary disaster. If a share shows you a good profit, do not let the effect of Capital Gains Tax put you off selling at least a proportion. Sharing the profit with the Inland Revenue has got to be better than watching it evaporate on the market.

The most successful investment I have ever made started in the most unlikely surroundings. I had been put in touch with an Australian schoolteacher looking for finance to publish a book about the Young Christian Workers. I was very busy at the time but had a free afternoon with only my third child to occupy so I suggested we meet in the fish department of the Natural History

Museum and so it was that while Elizabeth was busy drawing sharks in the corner I agreed to incorporate Geoffrey Chapman Ltd.

The first book performed to budget and we went on to publish another seven. I put it to Geoffrey that he give up teaching and become a publisher on the same pay. His wife Sue with a First in English from Melbourne University proved a powerful editor and between us we managed to do quite well. We eventually became involved with the Vatican Council and our real coup was obtaining the rights to publish Pope John's diaries. Of course we had to finance much bigger runs and I had to persuade the family's bank to be my guarantor. Some months later after we had finished The New English Liturgy, we received a takeover bid which made a huge profit for both our families on an issued capital of £2,200. I remember at the time pointing out to Tom Burns who ran our main competitors that, under English Law, 'an agreement to agree is not an agreement'.

Dermot's father and Bernard Baruch in Vichy.

Dermot and colleagues with Cheetah on a farm north of Lusaka, Zambia.

Dermot with founder members of Lincolnshire and South Humberside Institute of Directors.

Dermot receiving the Queen's award from the Duke of Norfolk.

Dermot speaks at press distribution lunch in Manchester.

East-West Trade

THE BEAVERBROOKS gave a dinner party for Andrew Parker-Bowles' 21st birthday, during the course of which I had a long conversation with a top French diplomat. We came to the conclusion that the only way to break down the East-West war was to, in his words, 'Il faut les enbourgoiser'; if people own a dacha they will start adopting middle class values.

Roland Berger, who ran the Association for the Promotion of International Trade, was a very easy companion and a paid-up member of the Communist Party (along with his wife) but, as I said to my managers, 'You are not going to meet the top people in the importing organisations through Conservative Central Office. Roland can organise this and the fact that they only charge a one-quarter percent commission on orders received as a result, obviously it is not used as a means of financing the Communist Party, even if Roland gives a large proportion of his salary. What you must be careful of is that it is a front organisation which is bound to indulge in industrial espionage and you should not tell them anything you don't want to tell the Kremlin'.

On my first visit to Moscow and I took with me my right-hand from the office who was Russian born and consequently a fluent Russian speaker. They managed to put us in different hotels and I had a very grand room with four marble columns but there was no plug for the basin, which I had been led to expect. The keys on each floor were retained by a fierce looking matron who would obviously report on all one's movements. I assumed my telephone line was bugged. Next day we had a meeting at Stanko Import which covered heavy machine tools. The Chairman's first remark to me was 'Why have we not heard from you before?' and I replied, 'Because we could not have quoted you a good enough delivery'. They did in fact need one of our vertical plate benders for their heavy electrical company, which made the turbines. We had dinner in one of the best restaurants where we were joined by a lawyer who explained that if anyone was put on a charge they liked to employ a personal lawyer, because that way they got better service. The waiter was rather slow in bringing our vodka and satisfied us with a little proverb, 'He who takes longest in saddling the horses gets furthest in the end'. The other remark worthy of mention was while we were waiting in the front hall for our first meeting. An old sweeper was reading *Pravda* and remarked in Russian, 'Emptiness, emptiness, nothing but emptiness'. We went to the Bolshoi Ballet production of *Swan Lake* in the small theatre. The ballerina came on flapping her wings and was greeted by rapturous applause from the audience. She was so good, (her name was Maria Vlasova which I'm told means Smith), that I wondered why we hadn't seen her in the West, presumably she was considered politically unreliable because at the time she was a hero of the Soviet Union 'second class'.

In Leningrad I was due to talk about four of my different companies, and their organisation was such that having fixed a time for my meeting in the morning, they all had to come representing all four products, which was rather boring for the cheapest items. They explained that with so many products being offered around the world, it was not possible to deal with component parts of equipment, only the whole thing. That eliminated valves and welding equipment but left voltage regulators as a borderline case.

Later I joined Trade Group's visit to Hungary which was most interesting. First we were taken for a weekend's partridge shooting at Nierekhaza and they had had some Italians shooting there before and when the birds got up all the beaters threw themselves flat, otherwise we might not have had so many beaters. On the Sunday morning one could see farmers and their wives driving in a cart to church, with the most beautiful horses. Our party consisted of Frank Perkins of the Diesel Engine Company, Bob Askwith of the Machine Tool Company, and Robson of Robson Morrow the Consultants. The following morning we got up at five o'clock to go goose shooting. Before going out we were given bread and peppers, which certainly woke one up. We shot a few geese but less than we should. Next day we visited the Czepel works which made everything from iron and steel to machine tools and bicycles. Their pillar drills were of very high quality as Bob Asquith himself confirmed. Conversation with the managing director was most interesting. In answer to the question could he, as MD, sack any employee?' I got, 'Yes, but they'd probably get a better paid job as a waiter'.

The state was in effect a participating preference shareholder who received a fixed return and then a proportion of what was left. The other half, if they made a surplus, was divided amongst the employees as a percentage of pay. Not surprisingly they had copied the Western habit of loading as much cost as possible onto a government development programme.

In London we had various dinners with the Foreign Trade representatives of the Eastern companies and I went off on a special visit to Warsaw to entertain the construction engineers from the three main shipyards, Dansik, Gdinya and Stettin, all of which had ordered our Hugh Smith machine tools. I kept the vodka circulating until late at night and had some difficulty negotiating my way out of the hotel into a taxi. I remember it being very hot and using the old naval expression, 'It is a long ship'. Meaning a long time between drinks.

Sometime later Eddie Shackleton, who was a Minister in the Lords and looking for other Labour Peers, asked whom I would suggest, and I immediately said our Chairman, Wilfred Brown, for whom I had very great respect as a forward-thinking employer. In due course Wilfred became a Junior Minister and I am told that when he read the confidential notes on Roland Berger he was very shocked. I said, 'I doubt it if anything about Roland would have shocked me'. Wilfred Brown, who was Chairman of Glacier Metals also chaired the Society for the Promotion of International Trade (with Iron Curtain countries).

Immigration

I HAVE ALWAYS BEEN an active campaigner for greater equality for immigrants in the UK and in 1967 I was asked to give a talk to the RSA in London on that subject in my capacity as a member of the National Committee for Commonwealth Immigrants. During that talk I estimated that by the end of 1967 the 'coloured population' of Great Britain would be at least one million strong and that industry and commerce should be prepared to absorb this growth in employment demand. I was keenly aware at the time of discrimination which occurred and still occurs and emphasised my opinion that a code of fair employment practice similar to that adopted in the United States would be essential if second generation immigrants were to get the opportunities they needed.

Britain has always benefited from immigration. In past centuries the Dutch wool trade and more recently, before the war, doctors and bankers of Jewish origin. When we were short of manpower on the buses we were very happy to train West Indians. Obviously immigration has to be controlled in numbers but once the immigrant is integrated into the British community, he must be given equal rights with other natives of these islands. The disadvantage of not doing so is that you waste talent and manpower and you create a disgruntled underclass. I was therefore very happy to serve on the National Committee for Commonwealth Immigrants and chaired the employment panel with the assistance of my friend, Jack Jones, then of the Transport

& General Workers Union. I will never forget the occasion when I arranged for Jack to meet me at the Institute of Directors, then in Belgrave Square. The Sergeant Major who ushered him into me could have been a Bateman drawing. Jack had problems because the established Irish dockworkers hated the new arrivals. In America I was very impressed by the progress that had been made by President Kennedy in his scheme *Plans for Progress* but I was infuriated by Enoch Powell's speech on the rivers of blood. He is too clever a man not to have known what he was doing and I decided that ridicule was the best answer so in 1969, in response to his ill-willed comments, I penned the following lines:

> Mad dogs and Englishmen must remain a race apart,
> Their slums will never stink,
> Their hair; without a kink,
> We all suppose
> Your flattened nose
> Results from the 'noble art'.
> Mad dogs and Englishmen must remain a race apart.
>
> Mad dogs and Englishmen must remain a race apart,
> The pigment of your skin,
> May not allow you in,
> Unless is came
> From sunny Spain
> Or that 'sterling' place Rabat.
> Mad dogs and Englishmen must remain a race apart.
>
> Mad dogs and Englishmen must remain a race apart,
> The fellow's made it plain,
> We'll have no racial stain,
> I can't construe,
> An English Jew,
> The ideas are Poles apart.

Mad dogs and Englishmen must remain a race apart.
Mad dogs and Englishmen must remain a race apart
The Irish, Welsh or Scot,
May join our jappy lot,
That yellow tinge
Is last night's binge
We can't have a Chinese Bart.
Mad dogs and Englishmen must remain a race apart.

10 Downing Street
Whitehall

December 1, 1968

Dear Mr de Trafford,

I am writing to express my sincere thanks for all you have done as a member of the National Committee for Commonwealth Immigrants which is now succeeded by the Community Relations Commission.

I am sure that the Commission will find that the Committee's achievements over the last three years have provided a sound basis for their future work. I hope that you will feel able to put your knowledge and experience at the Commission's disposal as occasion arises in the future.

Yours sincerely,
Harold Wilson

Dermot de Trafford, Esq.

Letter to Dermot from Harold Wilson regarding National Committee for Commonwealth Immigrants.

Sailing

M<small>Y LOVE OF THE SEA</small> stems from eight transatlantic crossings as a child and an unforgettable Mediterranean cruise in 1938. Throughout my life the sea has provided many sources of recreation for me; from the re-rigging and use of a Turkish fishing boat and dinghy racing in Alexandra Harbour to sailing on the Regents Park pond with our chauffer (also a great friend). Numerous holidays at Ardmore in Ireland provided various fishing expeditions and instilled in me a love of the sea and all things aqueous. I remember catching mackerel in the bay and sometimes so many were caught that they had to be used as manure.

At the end of war, having bought a house near the river with its own mooring at Beaulieu, Hampshire, I was determined to get a boat. There was a boat for sale of which I liked the sound and asked my mother to look at it on my behalf. Unfortunately all she could tell me was that it had a solid fuel burning stove and very pretty curtains. My question as to what condition the sails were in was not satisfactorily answered but I threw caution to the wind and bought the boat anyway. *Jeanne* was a thirty-foot Hillyard double ender with a Norwegian canoe stern. I have reason to believe she must have been over at Dunkirk because I came across a rusty old French rifle in the bilges. However she does not show up on any of the records and I never found any further evidence.

A memorable cruise before I sold *Jeanne* was a visit to Brittany

Silver Maid.

Dermot aboard a dragon.

Orthos. *Courtesy of Beken of Cowes.*

Myth of Malham. *Courtesy of Beken of Cowes.*

Kayak.

up the Treguier River to tie-up opposite the Hotel Lalausze. The day before we were going the manager asked would we like to take some oysters with us and if we did he would arrange for another fisherman to row out with them if we stopped just before the entrance to the river. This we did and we received the oysters, paid the fishermen, and heard a shot from the opposite bank. I pulled the throttle full ahead and told everybody to duck and we sped out of the river a full clip having been fired at us. I was not surprised when the Customs came on board in Jersey but the next I heard of it was from the French Consul in Southampton who informed me that in my absence I had been fined, I think a hundred thousand francs, and my boat was forfeit. So I replied, explaining the circumstances, and writing in my most colloquial French with much reference to the 'Relations Franco-Bretanique' and I was then asked if I was prepared to pay costs. The costs turned out to be some miniscule figure, I think it was six francs and some centimes, which I duly put in an envelope when next in Brittany and posted them to the Dounes. I have a receipt, the cost of which must have been more than the money sent.

Jeanne and I made our first voyage to Ardmore with three very good friends of mine as crew: Gurth Addington and Peter Loveband, both Oxford contemporaries of mine, along with our RC Catholic Chaplain, Monsignor Valentine Elwes, who had been a naval chaplain and was a perfect addition to the our merry band.

We sailed without major incident to the Scilly Isles and having rounded these successfully we put in to Padstow. Unfortunately we ran aground just opposite the harbour entrance, at which point a rather self-satisfied old man rode across and said unnecessarily 'There's deeper water over here'. To which I replied, tight-lipped, 'I know'. Eventually we made it into to the harbour and ashore for a meal.

All was well until our return from Ireland was seriously delayed by a car accident. We had piled into a large estate car belonging to Clem Magnier to go to the circus in Clonmel after a dinner in town with several of our contemporaries. My cousin Julian had not been drinking so we suggested that he should drive. All was fine until our descent down one of the steep hills where we developed a tail swing with all the weight in the back and went off the road, rolling down to the verge below and just missing a tar machine which would probably have killed several of us. Julian, the driver, had a collapsed lung, I had a gash in my wrist and there were various other minor casualties. Clem Magnier managed to get his brother, Dr Magnier, onto the scene and in his surgery I had my wrist sewn up without anaesthetic, the most painful experience I can imagine, all nerves passing through. Fortunately Ethne Dwyer, now Brabazon, next to me was unhurt and Gurth opposite seemed to be alright.

Shortly afterwards Clem wanted to sue Julian for the cost of the vehicle, which was not properly insured and I was able to sort it all out with the help of a cheque. Peter Loveband worked happily with Clem in his training stables after he came down from Oxford. Anne eventually married Julian with me as best man. Sadly Peter later drowned after his car drove off the end of a quay in Clonmel. I can just hear Peter saying, 'Fancy being drowned in the Suir (sewer) *and* on my birthday'.

As a result of our car accident in Clonmel, Peter and Gurth were unable to join us for the return sailing but I was lucky enough to get my Uncle Jacky and his good friend Robin Sinclair, an early member of the Royal Ocean Racing Club, to come and join us in Ireland and bring the boat home. I remember a particularly rough passage when he was acting as cook and decided that we had to have a white sauce with our peas – something which I had never had before…or since.

After several successful journeys on *Jeanne* and being sold on the merits of ocean racing, I joined the Royal Ocean Racing Club and decided that I was going to change boats. I was lucky enough to get one, *Kayak*, designed by Jack Laurent Giles, a so-called Channel Class.

Kayak was cutter rigged and worked well to windward but she was heavy because her previous owner who had seen her built and who had apparently infuriated the builders by his meticulousness had insisted on grown oak frames every third and mahogany planking, which was so beautiful that even the inside of the hull was varnished. We never made a great impression racing but she was a very comfortable boat.

Our first big race was from Plymouth to La Rochelle, where we met the larger boats that had been to Santander. I could hardly contain my excitement at the dinner after the race at being placed to the French film star Arletty, star of *Les Enfants du Paradis* and other French classics. Meanwhile I had been elected to the Royal Yacht Squadron. This was to some extent due to our neighbour Philip Hunloke, the King's former Sailing Master who in fact gave me a copy of *Lloyds Register* with the gold title 'HM The King'. Lord Campden, known as Brecky, was one of my sponsors and I got one of the old timers to second me. It was after that I did some competitive racing at Cowes and I was invited by Philip Colville whose family have a great history of racing to share a dragon with him. It so happened that Rob Hudson had just become a minister and so we bought his boat.

We had a very successful season, the height of which was in Cowes Week when we were leading on the last day but lying about fourth which wasn't good enough to win the prize. Accidentally we actually did the best thing to ensure winning, which was to sink and the other boats turned back to rescue us. It was a little scary at the time because we had a spinnaker set that had to come down, lowered by a paid hand who couldn't swim, and went forward to do the necessary, slipped over the side and was caught by the scruff of the neck by Philip but at that time I was busy trying to prevent us from being dis-masted and putting the runners up. I thought Philip was panicking when he passed me a lifebelt. Anyway before we could say Jack Robinson she'd gone and sailed under with no time to put on the lifejacket. Then this hand came up from the waves and I remembered my lifesaving drill by which one more or less knocked the poor fellow out and then dragged him ashore. I thought if I did that I'd drown him. The other fear was that Philip would have got a coil of rope around his ankle and I would have to duck dive to free him. Fortunately he emerged like a reverse shot in *Kind Hearts and Coronets* with his cap at the correct angle. He just bobbed up and I heaved a great sigh of relief. People came back to pick us up and the race was cancelled. And so we won the prize for Cowes Week. When we eventually got to the platform Brecky merely said, 'You got rather wet today, didn't you'.

We were supposed to be part of a team going over to La Havre to race against the Belgians and to my very pleasant surprise Jack Raymond who was the Class Captain and had been one of our rescuers said we could borrow his boat instead. Having just sunk our own this was rather valiant of him. So with naval escort we set out across the Channel in our little dragon. The weather was very kind and the Belgians were suffering from considerable inhibitions in that they never dared protest against the King's boat, regardless of what his Sailing Master did. We were not so squeamish and my white handkerchief was tied to the shroud when His Majesty's boat infringed the port and starboard rule very clearly. Fortunately he retired rather than be dismissed, which was a relief.

These were the highlights of my time with the dragons and after that I wanted to back a new Class, the South Coast One Design, which a number of friends were going into. These were being built up beyond Hayling Island. Most of the boats were called after various food or drink and I named mine *Éclair*, having just recently had a daughter called Clare. Robin who had helped us to bring the boat back from Ireland always used to call boats our 'wooden women' because we love them so much. The family's time with the South Coast One Designs was very undistinguished but at that time I was asked by John Illingworth, Commodore of the Royal Ocean Racing Club, whether I would be prepared to share *Myth of Malham* for the season. The real thrill for me was to win a race when I was commanding the boat and I had a very scratch crew – one semi-professional American, a very competent girl dinghy sailor, a very good sailor who lived at Beaulieu near us and my dear Uncle Jack. The first mark we had to round was a buoy numbered H10 in those days off Cherbourg and it was interesting because we couldn't at that time quite fetch it and I thought 'Well, we want to keep up to weather as much as we can'. Now I remember doing a race like this once before when the wind shifted later on and we were freed up. As a result of this we did extremely well and got round among the first. I was particularly racing against the Gunners' boat, St Barbara, and Fandango which was Major Gerald Potter's new one. Having listened to the weather forecast I banked on the fact that any wind that night would be coming offshore and stood right in to the English Coast. This proved to be right but the real winning stroke was when we got off the Edison Lighthouse and had to turn in for Plymouth. I suddenly realised that the wind which should have caused the tide to be ebbing had failed to do so and we were able on our first tack to round the Edison, and win the race by about twenty minutes on corrected time. It was

Lady Barbara Bossom aboard Silver Maid.

really exciting to win because it was a feeling of responsibility having John Illingworth's great boat.

Another experience of sailing with John Illingworth was when he built a boat for the Junior Offshore Group which he appropriately named *Mouse of Malham*. He'd had what was euphemistically described as kneeling headroom. And myself, having served as cook/navigator and watch-keeper I was on my knees a lot of the time. Gianni (Pera) who was on watch with me was the more senior, so needless to say I had to go forward every time for sail changes. We did the first Junior Offshore Group race together and the experience of Sopranino showed what very small racing yachts could do. John had rigged *Mouse of Malham* as yawl with an international mainsail as a mizzen which existed purely in order to hoist a mizzen staysail, an area of sail not penalised by the rule. Although we won our class, we never had a chance to hoist the mizzen staysail once, the winds went round ahead us after we turned round the Fastnet.

One of my most enjoyable sailing expeditions was a two week family cruise in the Skagerrak in 1957. To have a mooring at Beaulieu, to enjoy cruising, and never to have cruised in Scandanavian waters was such an obvious omission that steps had to be taken to correct it. A straight passage across the North Sea with a crew whose average age was sixteen was too risky an undertaking and the alternative of coastal passages was too time-consuming so the answer seemed to be to ship our Ocean Bird class trimaran *Triarch* from Tibury to Gothenburg aboard the m.v *Saga*. This operation proved somewhat costly but entirely satisfactory. I kept a daily diary throughout the cruise, which is reproduced below.

FAMILY CRUISE IN THE SKAGERRAK

Tuesday 6th August

The Skandia island terminal of Swedish Lloyd has a mammoth travelling crane, which on the first day of our passage chose to misbehave. Almost before a new coat of anti-fouling had been applied (three hulls somehow seemed to take longer to paint than one) a mobile crane had been provided. We and our mast were deposited in our appropriate positions just before 13.30 and with hulls still swung in, we motored off across the main channel to the yacht harbour of Långedrag.

The glass was high and the weather reminiscent of a September day in the Mediterranean. A swim before lunch was a must. We anchored outside Långedrag, but some small boys soon indicated that we would be in the way of the local ferry, so we moved on to anchor off Salth.

After a leisurely lunch, we motored back to the Shell fuelling jetty at Långedrag, on the starboard hand as you enter. Shell could not provide fresh water, so we moved to the jetty by the white tower, where we found a hose for our convenience. (Note to Shell: BP fuelling jetties invariably had a fresh water point).

We anchored outside Långedrag, this time clear of the ferries, to swing out wings, bend on sails and adjust the rigging. This earned us another swim, and tea.

At 17.40, with main and genoa drawing in a light westerly breeeze, we weighed and sailed slowly back along the shipping channel, having to tack just before 19.00 north of Kuskärsb Light, in order to avoid *Saga* on her return journey.

A few minutes later the breeze died away and we motored up past Skäddan Light, south of St Porsh and L. Varh. Off L. Varh we gave a tow to two small boys becalmed in a sailing dinghy, and at 20.30 we anchored in 1^1/$_2$ fathoms in a large bay off the north-east side of Björkö, four cables south of Ängh.

After supper we enjoyed a superb cloudless night, flat calm, lit by a harvest moon. A wonderful start to our cruise.

Wednesday 7th August

Saw us awake early, unaccustomed as we were to the short nights. Breakfast was eaten at what would normally be considered the unearthly hour of 07.00. Soon after 08.30 we were away, under all plain sail. We rounded Gallskärsb and set the spinnaker. The wind was force 3 from the south-west, and the barometer still reading 1020 millibars. By now we were getting used to the drill of leaving all red marks to the north or west, and all black marks to the south or east. It was a perfect morning for sun-bathing and photography, and for running under spinnaker past countless rocky islands.

I had been told that the back way into Marstrand was interesting. Fortunately the spinnaker had had to come down as we altered course to the westward, and under full genoa we sailed into a passage so narrow that another Ocean Bird coming in the opposite direction could not have passed. At the very end of the narrows, the wind came ahead, and we had to start the engine.

At 11.10 we picked up a mooring in the bay north-east of Marstrand. I had hardly stepped ashore before the Harbour-master asked me to telephone Swedish Lloyd. (This turned out to be about arrangements for our return journey). I could not help being impressed by the efficiency with which officials manage to keep track of the myriad of small yachts moving up and down the coast. We made use of the water tap and all the shopping facilities on the front, and then treated ourselves to lunch at the hotel at the far end.

After lunch the family got into conversation with one of the summer visitors, who was kindness itself and insisted on providing us with ice, a book of plans of Swedish anchorages and moorings, and some extra water. When I gathered he was just waiting for Ingrid Bergman to arrive, I was very tempted to develop engine trouble. Unfortunately 'Henry' (Ford) started without hesitation and in twenty minutes we found ourselves in a delightful cove for a swim. Jellyfish had started to appear and not all members of the crew were convinced that the white ones would not sting.

An hour later we motored out, and then set sail to clear Åstol. The wind had fallen light, we tacked slowly round Tjornekalv and up the channel east of Kladesholmen, then north up the channel from Marresk, until we bore away east and anchored in a bay three-quarters of a mile east of the northern tip of Flatholmen. On the Swedish chart this appears to be an obvious place to anchor (indicated by a nice circle of pale blue). We should never have picked it out on the Admiralty Chart.

We had no sooner anchored than two small boys in minute sailing dinghies came to investigate us. They would have been even more surprised if they had seen us after dinner settling down to a rubber of bridge

Thursday 8th August
Another perfect day, hence breakfast at 07.00. As there was hardly a breath of wind and the breeze appeared to get up after 08.30 we decided to go ashore and explore. Compared with the barren rocks of the coast, the green fields inland and the holiday cabins discreetly tucked away provided a delightful contrast.

Just before 09.00 we sailed, escorted by the two small boys who had now been joined by Father in a typical Scandanavian fishing boat with outboard. We continued the passage through the various narrows. At Hjärterösund, our escort left us. At Bockholmsund we saw a house that appeared to have slid into the water. In Kyrkesund we met a largish motor vessel, inevitably in the narrowest part of the channel, at a time when we had only just got steerage way.

The wind had now veered north-west and as the channel swung westward we had to start the engine. We then headed into the wind, passing between Skäddan and Libarna, passed round the west of Slubbersh and anchored in the large bay on the west side of Mollön. Anchored in nearly five fathoms, we left the centreboard down and used the opportunity to remove the remaining barnacles. The diving mask had the additional advantage of enabling the wearer to earn other bathers of the approach of jellyfish.

After lunch, with the wind still in the north-west, we motored to Måseskär, off the northern point set sail and were able to clear all dangers. Off Härmanö Huvid we eased sheets for Hättan in pursuit of a German yacht which we had last seen off Flatholmen. The wind freshened and off Gaso we passed our rival, only to be repassed by him later when the wind fell light. A flukey wind enabled us to get ahead again and eventually, without starting the engine, we secured alongside the southern outside wall of the yacht harbour of Lysekil. In a trimaran, unless the wings are swung in, one is hesitant to occupy special spaces reserved for guests, for the simple reason that the buoys for securing one's stern are too closely spaced. Indeed, during the whole of our cruise, we never saw another multihull.

Elizabeth and I found a supermarket not far away and we were off again shortly after 17.00 gooseswinging our way to Brandskär, the wind having swung round to the east.

At Brandskär there were yachts in all the favoured berths, and although we anchored with a line ashore, we were in danger of fouling some fishermen's nets. Apart from this, the gull colony (presumably attracted by the catch in the nets) were unduly vociferous. After a short exploration ashore, I bowed to the crew's union and motored round to the east side of Tån, where we anchored in eight fathoms, securing our stern to a ring ashore. This proved to be a very comfortable berth, but was not a position I would have chosen to occupy in a blow.

Friday 9th August
With only four fathoms of chain on the anchor warp, I am always slightly anxious about anchoring in deep water. However, for a calm night ours proved a very good berth. The presence of

increasing numbers of Portuguese men of war (do they feed on the jellyfish?) inhibited an early morning swim, but it was such a beautiful morning that I thoroughly enjoyed a bath in the cockpit with a bucket before the others were up. No wonder we ran out of water!

Following our usual fair weather routine, we weighed soon after 08.00 and in a light north-easterly sailed slowly north-westwards between the Malmöbrotten Marks. By this time we had finished cleaning ship and decided to set a spinnaker. By the time we rounded South Åstabrott, the wind had veered a little and we were able to carry the spinnaker right up the channel, lowering it as we altered course west to Smögen, where we sailed alongside at 10.30.

We had selected the first free berth, normally used by fishing trawlers, almost opposite the fish factory. This had the advantage that we were able to buy ice, fresh shrimps (recently cooked) and cold drinks in a sales department, which we found at the back. A short walk along the quay, and 100 yards up to the right there was an excellent self-service store. The water tap was just beyond the bend of the quay, set 50 yards back and as there was a space opposite, we shifted berth.

Smögen was full of Swedes on holiday and friendly fishermen. The sun was shining brightly. When we slipped under sail at 11.45, it was agreed that it was a place to which we would all willingly return.

We took the channel south of Kleven and at 12.30 anchored in the small bay to the south of S. Buskär.

This was clearly the island where the holidaymakers came to swim and sunbathe. Those wearing swimsuits appeared to be a small minority.

There were shoals of jellyfish round *Triarch* and Elizabeth said that she would prefer to prepare lunch. With the two boys I went ashore in the dinghy to find a patch of clear water in which we were relatively successful. With the aid of the goggles I swam a zigzag course, avoiding the thicker concentrations and seeing at the bottom the most beautiful variety of coloured starfish I have ever seen. There were also lovely big fish in shallow water and I made a note to bring a harpoon gun on any future visit to these waters.

After an excellent lunch of cold meats and iced beer bought in Smögen, we sailed before our drowsiness overcame us, taking the channel east of Buskär. Twenty minutes later I nearly blamed the beer for seeing a man standing on a small red buoy. I wonder what the bet was and how long he had to stay there.

The afternoon had brought a light westerly and by the time we reached Mjölskär Light we decided to find an anchorage for the night in Scotskär. At 16.00 we anchored in the lovely bay south of the twin main islands, in four fathoms. A Swedish yacht was anchored at the head of the bay with a line ashore and the family swam over for a chat. They sailed soon after our arrival. There were few jellyfish and good swimming and rock formations to explore ashore. The sun still shone on the outer islands but inland dark cumulus had piled up, from which we heard the occasional grumble.

In the Log I noted ' "a lovely anchorage" but a lee shore in a sou'wester, and open to it. Mares' tails at sunset suggest wind'.

Saturday 10th August
Sure enough, when I awoke soon after 05.00 there was a lovely fresh breeze from the sou'west. Having prepared the main and spinnaker, I called John, but the engine would not start. One plug was damp, two others were ungettable with a box spanner (belonging to the outboard). The fuel pump and distributor were cleaned in succession, but I only succeeded in flattening the

battery. The wind was freshening and the sooner we sailed off our lee shore the better. At 06.23 we passed outside the Gramja Rock off the north of the island and after Skagga we decided to set the spinnaker and suffered a small tear in hoisting against a sharp edge which we had omitted to tape. The glass had come slowly down to 1010, it was lowing force 4 from the sou'west, a marvellous reaching wind. The obvious thing was to set course for Norway.

Without an engine we needed somewhere with a front and back door and good garage facilities. Stavern looked perfect, and so it proved. By 08.00 we were off Vaderobod and set course for the Svenner Light.

At 11.50 I sighted the Foerder Light. Unaware of the extreme range at which it is visible, I looked on my large scale chart for another light which it might be and foolishly picked the Sydostgrunden Light Buoy. The resulting running fix caused me to alter course 20 degrees to starboard, and by the time I had realised my mistake we were not far from the Lysog Lydboie Buoy, so that for an hour we had to sail close-hauled to the westward. At 13.45 we passed inside the Dypeskoten Buoy and altered course for Stavern Light. The angle from which we approached this light looked like two houses. In contrast, the Minnehall, a great big pyramid, was clearly visible, but we could not be certain of the identification. At 14.23 we anchored in 3 fathoms in the bay south of Stavern.

Going back over my navigational errors I found that apart from the alteration of course based on a wrong identification, we had made 10 degrees of leeway instead of the 5 which I had allowed. I was not certain whether to blame 'George', the automatic steering vane who was used throughout the passage or a set up along the coast caused by the sou'wester. I subsequently came to the view that it was probably the latter.

Having anchored well clear of the town, our Johnson outboard was needed for the first time. Thank goodness it behaved with its customary reliability. Thereafter it was affectionately referred to as 'Oscar'.

Stavern proved to be pleasant with a slightly middle western flavour and largely consisted of white painted wooden houses. Our shopping expedition was entirely successful except that we could npt find where to buy ice. The garage proprietor of the fuelling jetty from whom we enquired insisted on giving us two trays for fee. He also sold ice creams and John and I enjoyed reciprocating by buying a shilling ice cream each.

Back on board I wrestled again with the main engine in vain and by now the battery was absolutely flat. So at 17.40 we sailed into the inner harbour and anchored in 3 fathoms south of the main jetty midway between it and a wooden jetty. Our anchorage was carefully selected because the wooden jetty has a water tap and is only 200 yards from the garage where we took our battery for charging. We noted for another visit that there is also a tap at the fuelling quay inside the main harbour. With only the riding light and torch light, we had every reason to go to sleep early.

Sunday 11th August

We awoke to a clear calm day. Breakfast not being served until eight, we had a real lie in. Liz busied herself ferrying water while Ned washed up. At 10.00 John and I picked up the battery and we all changed to go ashore, our aim being to walk to Larvik. The walk to the edge of town took an hour and twenty minutes. At various points we found footpaths which provided short cuts. Traffic was fairly heavy and the verges were somewhat narrow, but wild raspberries grew abundantly in the hedgerows and on one short cut we found some wild strawberries. Between the main quay and the station stands the Grand Hotel, which is very comfortable and sets out to please.

The hotel served us quite a good lunch but we were not allowed any spririts.

A quick phone call to Beaulieu to report all well and we caught the two o'clock bus back to Stavern. Although by the time we arrived the glass had dropped to 1005.5, it was a clear sunny day with the wind force 3 from the sou'west so we decided to sail to Rauane, where some cousins of ours normally spent their summer holidays.

Urged on by a freshly charged battery, the engine started. At 14.45 we weighed, hoisted the sail and cut the engine while we beat out to the south of the Light Buoy which marked the south east corner of the rocky shoals. We stood on southwards until 15.50 when we came about hoping to clear Tvistein. At that point we decided to take the inshore passage north west of Straahl and Jomfruland because we would have to motor in any case in order to arrive before dark and this route was calculated to have us motoring into the wind in calm waters. By 16.35 Tvistein was abeam and an hour later we started the passage through the Narrows. This entailed careful piloting with alterations of course every few minutes, but it was a beautiful evening with the landscape rural but well cultivated, reminiscent of Switzerland. Although I had plotted all courses and distances, we had one or two mirage effects and I find it better to bring the chart on deck Furthermore, we had discovered a compass error of some 10° west, which had to be added to 3° of variation. This error was not apparent when sailing and I guessed that it was due to a new generator which had been fitted on the engine. By 18.30 we were due west of Straaholmhode. Half an hour later we passed through the narrows of Djupodden. A few minutes later we rounded the Midtfjordkj rocks and stopped to review the situation. The

Rauane Islands looked nothing like the sketch which I had been given by my cousin (understandably, because I was looking at East Rauane and she had given me a sketch of West Rauane), however we proceeded with care and anchored in a patch of clear water east of the northern islet. With no room to swing, we put out the ketch aft and I rode ashore to be informed that the Viborg family houses were on West Rauane. I was advised to move to a more comfortable berth north of the main island, but I had no sooner got round there than another kind friend shouted to us to move into his harbour on one of the west islands. At 20.30 we finally anchored in his bay and moored with the help of Mr Stange's son. Their house is marked on the chart and is the old pilot house.

After we had eaten, he and his wife came aboard for a drink and insisted on returning on returning our hospitality most fully. They kindly telephoned to book rooms for us in Olso and their two pretty daughters provided convincing reasons for the boys to want to return in a few years' time. It was 23.00 by the time we all got to bed, after a most enjoyable day rounded off with a wonderful evening.

Monday 12 August
The barometer had dropped to 1002.4 and by 08.30 the wind was northerly with a light drizzle. We went ashore to say 'hallo' and 'goodbye' to our hosts and to double the lines for slipping.

At 10.20 we slipped and 22 minutes later we anchored in the anchorage marked on the Norwegian charts in the middle of West Rauane. By now the rain had cleared and the glass was rising, but we were disappointed on going ashore that the Viborgs had left the previous day. The morning was spent quietly reading and playing chess and by noon the sun had come out.

After a satisfying lunch of Father's best paella, the two main islands were explored. My presence on one of them was most unpopular and a pair of seagulls carried out some very effective dive bomb attacks straight out of the sun. This had its desired effect and at 14.40 we weighed under all plain sail, to sail round Krageö. It was a most beautiful afternoon and I took the opportunity of taking photographs of the boat from the dinghy which we were towing.

We anchored off the town at 15.35 and went ashore to shop and send off postcards. We liked the town, which was well provided with shops and appeared to be more commercial than Staven. Before leaving we went alongside the south east side of the harbour for fuel and water and by 16.30 we were away again, this time setting course between Berö and Skaatö. The scenery was perfect, rather like the lake country of Quebec with lots of scattered little wooden shacks.

As we approached the Narrows of Sauö we went to the rescue of a man and his daughter with a fishing boat with a broken down outboard. A rainstorm had just started so we took them aboard and gave them a hot tea while we towed their boat to Rytterholme, where they were staying. By the time we arrived the rain had stopped and they rode on while we went and anchored southwest of the island in the bay north of Braaten.

We had a swim and cleared everything up and all set off in the dinghy to explore Gumö. We had an excellent ramble all over the Kjelsö Peninsula and returned just before the next shower with a large bunch of white heather.

Supper was followed by a long rubber of bridge and we all retired very sleepy at 23.00.

Tuesday 13 August
Dawn fine and clear, but the glass had dropped to 1001.2 and by 10.00 it had clouded over. We followed the buoyed channel north

of Rytterholme and south of Oterö round the northern end of Jomfrüland, where at 11.00 we hoisted sail and stopped the engine. Once again we passed south of Tvistein passed the lifebuoy south of Stavern and altered course for the Sciboen pillarbuoy. The wind was now southerly force 3 and at 14.00 the spinnaker was set but although the glass had dropped further, the weather was clearing. Following the pllarbuoys to enter Sandefjord, the afternoon grew hotter and the boys stripped to the waist. At 15.00 we passed to the east of Flaten and dropped the genoa. It was a dead run up to the fjord and we had to gybe twice. At 16.00 we anchored in a temporary berth, in order to get ashore before the shops closed. Unfortunately, only the tobacconists stay open after 16.00. There was some consolation for us in the fact that they also sell fruit. This was the largest town we had visited in Norway, with excellent shops and a Vin Monopolet on the quay which we noted for suture occasions. The three large hotels make this a popular conference centre and the rich rewards brought in by the whaling fleet no doubt accounts for the number of banks. Because the whaling fleets sail for the Antarctic summer, they spend the northern summer refitting in port. On the front there is a very fine bronze fountain reminiscent of the days of Moby Dick. The guide book informed us that one and a half million tons of shipping is registered in Sandefjord and that the annual receipts of the whaling industry amounts to as much as £7,500,000. But we had come to Sandefjord not for the charms of the town itself but to get on to Olso.

At 17.00 we moved to the small boat harbour, where we anchored with our stern to the piled. The width between them was too narrow even with our wings swung in.

Wednesday 14th August
We awoke to steady rain which continued until late afternoon.

After breakfast we piled into a taxi and caught the train at 09.11 having just had time to cash some travellers cheques at the bank opposite the station, which opened at 09.00.

On arrival at Oslo station we bought a map and decided to walk to the Savoy Hotel. Unfortunately, the station was not very clearly marked on the map and our routes somewhat circuitous. By the time we arrived the kitbags were feeling very heavy.

Lunch in the hotel sustained us for tours of the historical museum, the National Gallery and an English comic film, *How I won the war*. That evening we had an excellent dinner at Frascati's. As Ned was leaving the following day, we agreed to his suggestion of a final rubber of bridge.

Thursday 15th August
An early start, as Edmund's bus left the SAS office at 08.00. This was fully compensated for by an excellent self-service breakfast.

At 10.15 Liz, John and I caught the ferry to Bygöines across the bay, where we saw the Kontiki museum (where the raft is preserved in a most realistic setting) after which we visited the Antarctic expedition ship *Fran*. We then walked round to Dronningen where several Viking ships are preserved in a museum; although beautifully preserved the ships are less impressive than the thought of the voyages undertaken in them. We took the ferry back from Dronningen and a bus back to the airport (as it is only fifteen minutes from town). As we were finishing an excellent lunch in the Caravelle restaurant, Mary and Clare arrived on time and in good order.

This time we all piled into a taxi, dropped their baggage at the station and went straight to the Munch museum. The museum, which is very modern, houses a superb collection of the work of this most interesting artist, which we were very glad not to have missed.

From the museum we managed to catch a bus going in the wrong direction, as the result of which we missed the train we had meant to catch . Instead we did our provisioning in Oslo which included a visit to the Vin Monopolet which was free of queues and gave excellent service. This gave us time to go back to Dronningen for a visit to the Norwegian Folk Museum, which we had had to miss out in the morning. Our visit was slightly curtailed and we managed to show Mary, who was studying Anglo Saxon, the Viking ships before we caught our ferry back to the centre of town and the next train to Sandefjord. Various snacks were served in the train but the day was rounded off by a big brew up of soup and cocoa, according to taste.

Friday 16th August
The glass was at its low point of the voyage at 998.4 but the weather looked reasonable. At 07.30 after a shower had cleared away, we went ashore to fill up with water from the tap which is located twenty yards to the right of the green landing stage. At 08.00 we motored out to the accompaniment of thunder and anchored in the bay west of Asneset light.

While the girls washed up breakfast we swing out the wings and at 09.40, with the wind in the North East, we hoisted sail and weighed. An hour later, off the end of the peninsula, the wind fell light and we had to motor between islands and the point. The course was initially set south of Tjömeboan islet but when the wind piped up from the south we altered course to pass south of Svartakj after which we set the spinnaker and followed the route north of Klövingen and south and east of Vasser. By noon we were off Kruke, we rounded the north of Vasser and anchored in four fathoms of Brötsö at 12.30. Unfortunately the spinnaker halliard had jammed and the spinnaker was flying out astern causing us to drag. John was winched up the mast and succeeded in freeing it. Having recovered the spinnaker we sat down to lunch without bothering to clean up on deck.

There appeared to be no shops on Brötsö, so we motored down the fjord to Vestgaard where we went ashore in the dinghy to walk to Kruke. In Kruke we noted a BP fuel station and a fresh water tap; at the post office there was a fish and chicken fryer and some stores, but the main store we discovered was south of the church.

We sailed from Vestgaard at 15.30 passing south and east of Vaskalven and anchored in the bay north of Bustein at 16.10.

This proved to be a very satisfactory uninhabited islet, well covered with vegetation and with some interesting rock formations. To the south east there was a bay which would give excellent shelter, although there is a tricky rock in the entrance. The glass was steady so I decided to put out a kedge to the south and hope for the best. My decision was reinforced by the fact that the engine would not start. Was the battery flat again?

That evening our rather expensive fried chickens, done up with cream, aquavitae and a game of poker, at which Clare was the winner, ended a very satisfactory start to the second half of the cruise.

Saturday 17th August
I was woken by the sound of heavy rain. By 05.30 the north east wind had raised a lop and swung us rather near to the rocks. The engine again refused to start so, wasting no time, I slipped the kedge and recovered it with the dinghy and weighed at 06.00 beating out fairly comfortably clear of danger. Before Ildverket we tacked and at that point the wind fell light and veered and we only just cleared the Svarten rock on the next leg.

The wind then freshened and backed north so that we were

able to set course well to weather of Struten. This was the point when porridge proves its worth, not that the subsequent eggs and bacon were any less acceptable. By now rain had been replaced by intermittent drizzle from a pale grey sky. Soon after 08.00 we passed Struten, getting a transit with the buoy. We eased sheets for Lynghl Island, passing to the north and anchoring at Papperhaven at 09.40 Liz and Clare were fast asleep. As usual there was a convenient water tap at the BP fuelling jetty and a man with a fair knowledge of English who was able to direct us to an excellent general store 100 yards up the road, where we did a thorough reprovisioning. As we needed no fuel (unfortunately) and no charge was made for water, we gave the attendant a bottle of beer. The rain had cleared by the time we reached the shop and after an hour's siesta we decided to sail for the Tisler Islands. The engine nearly started. Sailing out of the western entrance presented no problem with a north wind. However, there are a good few knobs about and I was quite happy to follow in the wake of a motor cruiser. We carried on southg and at 15.50 altered course to 150° and set the spinnaker. We passed about 4 cables off Tresteinene at 16.40 with the wind dropping with Alne abeam we lowered the spinnaker and anchored in 2 fathoms in a position indicated on the chart 020° from Molo beacon at 17.43. After a short exploration of the island we met two fishermen who had had a good day and pressed two excellent codling on us which were duly eaten with a cheese which became too like a fondue for comfort.

Sunday August 18th
With the glass at 998 and a nice breeze from the NNE, I noted that the day looked like 'showers and bright intervals'. In fact we never had any rain. Our rudder had come a little closer to the rocks and I thought it would be simpler to get underway under

genoa only, so I passed the anchor warp to the stern and brought our line from the shore to the bows, to the considerable disturbance of those sleeping below.

Shortly after 09.30 we sailed, passed outside Startsfkjne and at 09.56 the courtesy flags were changed as we re-entered Swedish waters. We passed close along the coast of Nord Koster, inside Morholmen, and the north of Bränd and Jutholmen, tacked around Hälsholmen (the large island east of Jutholmen) unnamed on chart 280a, and anchored in the bay, 3 cables north-west of the island, with the kedge out, at 11.20.

After lunch, propelled by 'Oscar', I dropped Mary and Clare for a walk on Nord Koster and returned to fetch John. Elizabeth offered to stay on board. A small adjustment to the warps caused our anchor to drag, so I moved the kedge to the starboard bow out at 45° to the main anchor, and with difficulty hammered a stake into the cleft in a rock to secure our stern. In such places, if there are no stakes or rings ashore it usually indicates bad holding ground.

The girls did not like Nord Koster much, so we crossed to Sor Koster, which we found to have a number of old-fashioned two-storey wooden houses, their gardens fenced all round, dotted higgeldy-piggledy in bare waste land. In contrast to most of the other islands the Kosters lacked charm.

Back on board, John was able to weigh the main anchor by under-running it with the dinghy. We sailed at 16.40, this time passing south-west of Halsholmen, down the channel inside Maskär and Vaskär. Transits on Ramskar light indicated 10° westerly deviation on the main compass, (which we knew) and 40° westerly deviation on the hand-bearing compass, which appeared to account for the rather large cocked hats. All dangers were so clearly visible that we sailed inside Brändeflu and 2 cables south of Kalvhättan, passed half a cable south of Kuongen at

18.15, followed the channel south of Ursen, and passed the red beacon between Lindoon and Resö. We turned east to go and anchor in $2^{1}/_{2}$ fathoms in the bay south west of the little island off south Resö near the landing stage. Once again we went ashore to explore. This proved to be a pleasant wooded island with a number of summer houses. We returned for a swim and a game of vingt-et-un. By the time we went to bed it was a flat calm and the glass had risen to 1003.2.

Monday August 19th
Awake at 05.30 so I removed the riding light and later heard the weather forecast. The glass had risen to 1007.0 and there was a light wind from the east.

After breakfast a fresh attack was mounted on 'Henry', which revealed that one of the jets was jammed in and could not be unscrewed and the cylinder head had water in it and the plugs were wet. Not surprisingly 'Henry' refused to start, so at 09.45 Liz and I set out for a shopping expedition in Havstensund in the dinghy. The wind by now was southerly and it took us 40 minutes to get there but only 30 to return.

Although there was a small village, we found an excellent 'Konsum' some 200 yards from the main quay. The quay itself had fuel pumps and a rather indifferent general store. It was a lovely morning and as pleasant a shopping expedition as anyone could wish. My spirits rose even higher when I returned on board to find everything spick and span.

Following an excellent cold lunch and a visit from three young Swedes, we weighed at 13.40. In view of the wind direction we had to retrace our steps; in light airs we ghosted between Lindön and Ursen, we then beat out between the islands very close to the twin isle of Svangen. The wind was now sou'west force 3 and the glass had risen to 1014.0. By 15.30 we were half a mile south of

Ramskär and we decided to tack inshore. I was working from a chart which had not been corrected since 1959, since when a number of new beacons had been built. South of Ulsholman we tacked out to sea, came in again on Morö and after another short tack we passed Brämskär half a mile to port at 17.23. At the time I noted the Fjelbacka spire was very prominent but hard to pinpoint on the chart. Perhaps it was because we very much wanted it so soon; without an engine it was far from certain whether we should make it.

A sou'wester was perfect for our purpose and carried us north of the Brottamgsk Rocks passed Lock Lökholm between Vallingsk and Grotsk south of the rock in the middle of the channel. We were being chased by a Swedish yawl which looked somewhat like a 12 metre, but we had managed to keep our lead; in light airs we passed south of Prosholm to see Fjellbacka gradually reveal itself to us. Perhaps one of the best moments of the whole cruise. At 18.30 we anchored west of the southern end of Krakh Island.

The first job was to give the battery an overnight charge. Even the tedium of carrying the battery right over the hill to the garage on the edge of town did little to detract from the pleasure of the evening. On our way we noted a bank and post office at the top of the hill and some useful shops. An inspection of the yacht harbour revealed very little room, the only space alongside was now taken by the Swedish yawl outside the wooden jetty east of the small boat harbour. The pork chops from Havstnssund were excellent. After a game of backgammon by torchlight we got to bed early.

Sunday 20th August
At 06.00 the sky was clear and there was a fresh offshore breeze. The barometer was back to 1019.8. We sent the girls off for a bath

at the Municipal bathhouse (*varmlad*), which apparently closed after 15th August and the two hotels were not cooperative. We found one tap for fresh water near the *varmlad* and we were also offered one in the basement of the *konsum* where we stored ship. I persuaded a young mechanic from the motorcycle repair shop to come and have a look at our engines; when he discovered we had water in the cylinder head he shook his head and wouldn't tackle it.

By now the wind had returned to the south west force 3 and after a hearty lunch on board we weighed at 14.10 turning the way we had come until we were north of Grötsk whence we beat down to Urskär light and at 14.41 passed through the largest gap between the chain of islands. An operation not to be recommended except in perfect visibility. South of Langeskär we tacked again , by 15.20 we were close abeam Södra Syster light. There appeared to be a north-going current so we tacked back inshore, the wind had fallen light and at 17.13 we rounded St Häskär with some difficulty, at 18.00 we passed south of Saltskär Vak between the rocks, rounded St Röskär, glided into the fjord north of Denmark and dropped the sails in an excellent anchorage in a bay south of the island north of Denmark. As usual, when without the engine, we had selected an anchorage with both a front door and a back door.

Denmark proved well worthy of exploration, rocks had been blasted from the hillside to build jetties, presumably for the benefit of holiday-makers and stonemasons. There were several good beaches and the hillsides were littered with wild flowers. White heather and honeysuckle are a very happy combination in the cabin.

Attempts to remove the cylinder head from the engine had failed owing to inadequate tools; it was clear that we were going to have to buy tools and do a major overhaul at the earliest possible moment. We retired early with the object of sailing at first light catching the offshore breeze.

Wednesday 21st August
At 05.45 the wind was south east, but despite the fact that the barometer had risen to 1024.0 there was a light drizzle. By 06.04 we were aweigh, for the third time running returning the way we had come. We felt our way between the rocks, south west of the western point of Denmark before coming close hauled. Our early start paid off and we were able to fetch Mjölskar which we passed at 07.17. Half a mile north of Långebrottet we tacked and on the next tack fetched through the passage between south Buskär and Vämlingen. Beyond Sälö seas were heavier and progress slower, the wind had veered 2 points. We had to do 3 tacks to clear the south Astabrott, by which time we had decided to make for Lysekil; the combination of one case of sea sickness, an overcast sky and steady drizzle, coupled with the need for repairs to 'Henry' made this an easy decision to take. At 09.50 we passed between the Malmbrötten marks, carried on to L. Kornö; our next tack carried us close in to Bogmästaren, the next tack not quite clear of Kornö Kalv so we had to put in a short one; two more tacks saw us pass the breakwater in Lysekil north harbour where we anchored at 11.12.

Ashore we met three most helpful Swedes who gave us a lift to the middle of town, No one had heard of a Ford agent, but we were able to by some superb Swedish tools and all the provisions we needed so that we were back on board by 11.50 and had the cylinder head dismantled before lunching at 13.00.

There was considerable corrosion which had to be cleaned away but the gasket was fortunately undamaged, everything went together again and despite the amount of oil everywhere 'Henry' started at the second attempt. At 15.36 we weighed and although there was some hesitation in the engine note, after motoring around for a few minutes we decided to hoist sail and proceed. We motored round to the south side of Lysekil, passed north of Toba island at 16.00. With the engine performing reasonably well and armed with a new set of tools should it misbehave, it seemed reasonable to take the inshore passage back, so we carried on to the east and rounded Gråbensk after which followed the most intricate pilotage which I had ever encountered. Off Hallsk we turned east and followed the slalom course through to Koljö fjord. Had I known the width of the passages between vertical rock faces and isolated rocks, I should certainly have swung the floats in.

By the time we entered the fjord, it was a most pleasant afternoon with the sun trying to come through the clouds. We hoisted sail and cut the engine, but the wind fell light and having restarted 'Henry' at 17.40 we passed the narrow passage between Bårholm and Goden, wending our way up the fjord which had now changed its name to Kalvo, until at 18.15 we passed under the Sundsandvik bridge. Even though I knew we had very wide clearance, there is always a moment of heightened tension, which took me back to my days in HMS *Dauntless* when twice a week we passed under the Forth Bridge. As we rounded the north of Orust we took the short cut to the west of the islands of Hasselom. At 19.06 we passed close south of Björingarna light and went to anchor in $1^{1}/_{2}$ fathoms in the bay north of Strande Island at 19.15. The last part of our passage was in the Havstens Fjord and a more lovely evening's motoring would be hard to imagine. The sun had come out, the weather was a little warmer and soft pastoral scenery unrolled on either side.

That evening the radio told us of the move towards liberalisation in Czechoslovakia. It seemed a fitting end to a most successful day. Lights out at 21.30 was not too early for anyone.

Thursday August 22nd

John and I were up at 06.45, a lovely morning with a light wind from the south-east, the barometer 1028. 'Henry' started at the first attempt and we weighed at 07.06 continuing our journey southwards. At 07.38 we entered the next narrows off Strandanäs light, passing Ejurnäsu light at 08.03 and Galteröm light at 08.35. At 09.00 we passed under a beautiful tubular steel bridge linking the little island of Kallön with Tjörn and by 10.25 we had reached the light of Älgön. Meanwhile, a complete clean-up of the ship was in progress and as we rounded the west coast of Koön it was spotless.

At 11.10 we stopped at the BP fuelling jetty north of Marstrand and then went and picked up a mooring near our old friend Mr Hill Lindquist. It was lucky that we caught him as he was already aboard preparing to leave. We were able to thank him for the loan of his book which had been of great assistance and to tell him a little of our cruise. The successful inside passage was celebrated by lunch at the hotel after which we returned on board with our shopping and sailed at 14.30. By now the wind was north west force 2/3 which enabled us to sail straight from our mooring, south of Ärholmen and between Ramholmen and Lönbäcken, at which point we set the spinnaker. Off Sälo we selected our anchorage for the night and made our way towards the northern point of Burö, sailed round to anchor between Långholm and Ängholm in $1^{1}/_{2}$ fathoms half a mile south of Burö.

Although landing on Långholm was not easy, there was plenty to explore and I have kept a souvenir in the form of a rather battered plastic bowl which had been washed ashore.

Friday August 23rd

Our last day at sea and the glass at an incredible 1034.5, wind light southerly, a fine day but a little light cumulus on the horizon. By the time we weighed at 09.45 it was flat calm, the anchor had to be disengaged from thick weed. We left our anchorage though the narrow passage to the south-east, then altered course south-west, rounding the northern point of Öckerö, rounded the west coast of Hönd, passing inside Hönöhuvud light and motored steadily on towards Gothenburg as we gradually prepared to stow everything away for the passage home. At 11.44 we anchored in a little bay just north of Knippelholm, rather conscious of the fact that there were electric power cables in the vicinity and hoping that we would well clear them. After an early lunch we weighed and twenty minute later we were at the ferry terminal lying under the gantry crane.

This time the crane was in working order and I couldn't help wondering whether it ever had as light a load as our little mast. *Triarch* was settled back onto her cradle and our friends in the shipping office booked hotel rooms for us in Gothenburg.

Although it seemed a pity that twenty four hours good cruising should be missed through having the boat ready for early loading, none of us regretted the twenty four hours we were obliged to spend in Gothenburg.

The Palace Hotel was perhaps most welcome for its hot baths and comfortable beds. We greeted civilisation by seeing a film, 'The Wild West' and balanced a visit to the fairground the following afternoon with a visit to the art museum in the morning. Gothenburg can indeed cater for every taste!

The glass was so high that I suspected an error but on checking with the Captain on the way home, I found that his barometer was reading 1035.

We were fortunate in many ways. The weather varied between the outstandingly good and the reasonably good, my lack of forethought on tools and spares for the engine caused no real hardship and there was a pleasant absence of unforeseen complications.

Even in less favourable weather conditions, I can think of few more enjoyable cruising grounds. None are superior in scenic variety or in the hospitality of the inhabitants to the visiting yachtsman.

I am too old and stiff for sailing now and the final insult was going round the island with one of my sons-in-law who, as I threw myself across the coach roof when we tacked, said, 'Dermot, that was a double axle with sulker but your feet weren't together'. Several of my children have got boats but I have refused invitations because I'm not quite sure whether I could climb over the guardrails any longer.

My final enterprise was to persuade Calor Gas to have a propane fired boiler in a Thames steamboat. I had seen the most beautiful lines in an old broken down hull, lying in Peter Freebody's yard on the Thames and persuaded Calor to build it into a steam yacht which as far as I know to be propane fired on the Thames. We had a lot of difficult rules to get over but it proved a great success and it now means that you can go straight out to sea, instead of doing what my son-in-law used to which was lighting a coal fire in the boiler, which usually takes over half an hour.

The steam yacht was very beautiful and I called her *Odile*, after the black swan in *Swan Lake*, and appropriately I had her named by a ballerina. She has appeared in various films and at the end of her commercial days I bought her from Calor and gave her to my son in law whose father, unusually, had a licence in steam.

Odile.

Dermot skiing in France.

Dermot, sons and oldest grandson on skiing holiday.

Skiing

My skiing holidays have been many, but I did not start going regularly until several years after I had first been skiing in Turkey. On one memorable occasion we chose a hotel in a village close to St Moritz under the shadow of the Bernina. One day whilst on an expedition we saw an avalanche come down the mountain , fortunately nowhere near us. After that I transferred my loyalty to Klosters where many of the German aristocracy have houses.

It was quite funny that I should go off with Fritz von Hohenzoller and his companions who were experts. Graf Rechtberg knew all the ways of going away from the main routes (off piste) and another member of our party was Koenigs Eck and his wife Putzi. Also at Klosters we used to see the Choremis. He, like me, had been at Le Rosey but was a far superior skier and Mariola, his wife, was also first class. It was the first time in my life that I had been on a helicopter to go skiing. I think it was Mariola's suggestion and it was great fun because we went straight up to a mountain which had then not yet been developed for skiing and came down in deep snow. The helicopter was owned by the same man who had the Head ski monopoly. I remember him as Walter. With a French daughter-in-law we naturally went to French resorts fairly frequently. Val d'Isere and Tignes stand out and I particularly enjoyed having younger members of the family learning to ski with me. Unfortunately there was a collision between my youngest daughter and her sister which ended in the youngster having a broken leg and we had to rush down in a bloodwagon. I accompanied her in a ski ambulance to the doctor's surgery. Fortunately it was not a bad break and we had brought the children's nurse out with us who was able to look after them.

On a couple of occasions I have been to Zermatt. I particularly enjoy going up the Monte Rosa, which is about thirty thousand feet, and skiing in the shadow of Matterhorn and then on down to Italy which was my first stop after the war. On one occasion my wife was more unlucky than me and, trying to follow her long legged friend through the snow, she pulled her knee, fell and was promptly guarded by a very fierce looking St Bernard, who wouldn't let anyone else approach. She was not encouraged on arriving at the doctor's surgery to be told that she was the hundredth case of 'knee' he had had that season.

The time I had my own case of 'knee' was quite ridiculous. I was on holiday in Verbier and meeting my companions for lunch. Admittedly I'd had a small carafe of white wine and a kirsch and skiing to the bottom of the lift after lunch I was too relaxed, suddenly did the splits and also did my knee! However, every situation has an advantage and while I was recovering I pored over a Russian phrase book and subsequently discovered to my advantage that many of the travel terms are the same.

This was prior to my first visit to Russia which I made under the auspices of the British Council for the Promotion of International Trade (with Iron Curtain countries).

Other Travels

(a) USA

I HAVE TRAVELLED to many parts of the world, both for business and pleasure (sometimes the two overlapping) and have been fortunate enough to meet a diverse and interesting range of people and to see many wonderful sights.

I have been to the USA on a number of occasions and one of my favourite cities is Washington. I suppose this has been largely because my stepmother had two nieces who live there and I am godfather to one of the sons, who married a delightful Argentinean girl, against the wishes of her father who has cut her off from all the family. (My own attempts at bridge building have sadly been useless). When in Washington one of my favourite pastimes is to visit the National Art Gallery and to see again the Mellon Collection with all the spectacular Turners. Unlike New York, Washington is short of performance stages but to my mind the Kennedy Center to a degree makes up for this in quality. Washington is also blessed with many fantastic restaurants and bars, always making for a satisfying and comfortable trip.

I have visited plants and refineries down the Mississippi throughout my career but my favourite stopping point has always been New Orleans. The hotel I always used to stay in had a swimming pool on the first floor level with a veranda leading to it. The cuisine in New Orleans is rather special but the highlight for me was always a visit to Preservation Hall where the paper is peeling off the walls and where you can still feel the presence of Louis Armstrong and his band. In fact while I was there, the remaining members of the band played along with Armstrong's replacement, in fifteen minute sessions. At the end of each session the front third would file out and those in front would fill the gaps. On one occasion the pianist had had a stroke and would only play with one arm; which she did with admirable dexterity. The double bass player was an old timer accompanied by a very blond Scandinavian on trumpet. Very *Streetcar Named Desire.*

I have always liked Chicago and I have many friends there who run the sports clubs and when I am there I am always made most welcome in their residences which have indoor tennis courts and other such luxuries.

I had a brother-in-law in LA and I always like to go to the Getty Museum, which apparently Paul Getty had never visited because he hated flying so much. A great friend of mine who lived nearby used to dine with Paul regularly and when I met him I found him to be a delightful companion about whom there are exaggerated rumours. I am however proud of teaching him one thing; the origin of the name of the wine Chateau Beychevelle when he generously ordered some at Anabell's. They still have the dipping sail, *baisse voile*, on the label and I was told that any ship that didn't dip to the owner of the fort on the point of the Girond would be fired at.

(b) South America

Balfour Williamson, the Merchant Banking end of the Bank of London and South America and shareholders in GHP, encouraged me to go and examine markets in their area. I started off in Peru, where I arrived to find the management having a drinks party with, it seemed to me, all of Lima. I made friends with a man called Julio de Grisolles who suggested that as it was the Easter weekend I should come and join him as guests of the President of the Banco Popular, Mariano Prado, on the Monday.

This I did, with two of his sons, and was much impressed by the beauty of Marianno's daughters. We had a very jolly time, and having found that Julio had been at school in Glasgow we were singing 'I belong to Glasgow' in the streets of Ancon. We then passed to the Yacht Club where I saw the most beautiful girl and said, 'she must have been a model'. 'Yes, she was Miss World 1953'. On the Tuesday I managed to persuade the shipyard who was building a Hunt destroyer, to order from us a cold frame bender.

My visit to Santiago de Chile was not so successful. Everybody was very busy with a visit from the Duke of Edinburgh who was being crowded by photographers and was reputed to have given a good backward kick, which kept them at a distance thereafter. However, I flew down to Conception, which was the naval base, and then took the Comet across to Buenos Aires. The Spanish accent there is abominable and I was sympathetic to my Peruvian friend who said to his friend in BA., 'I always take my holidays in New York because there I can understand the language'. The one thing I learned from my friend in BA was how to exist with very high inflation; you must owe lots of money and not be owed any.

(c) Japan

One of my most interesting journeys was to Japan, a country that I found more 'foreign' than any other. Our visit in April 1982 was organised by PA consultants in order to study productivity. In Tokyo the cherry blossom was just beginning and I was amazed at the habit of some Japanese to take their tatami rugs and a bottle of spirits and lie down under the trees and get absolutely plastered. We made some excursions North and it was amazing to see that the waterfall at the end of Lake Nikko Kogon was still absolutely frozen. The factory visits we made were extremely interesting. In the sewing machine factory in Nagoya the workers stood on different size boxes to bring them up to the right height.

In the Toyota bodyworks I saw a marvellous subject for the late Heath Robinson. The sides of vans were coming off a vertical press and there was a danger of them falling backwards instead of forwards. To solve this problem someone had taken a broomstick, wrapped some rubber around it and ingeniously suspended it from two ropes in front of the press so that as the sides came off they tapped against the rubber and fell the right way.

During that visit we had a weekend off and took the high-speed train from Tokyo down to Kyoto. We stayed in a western style hotel, not fancying the idea of sleeping on a wooden pillow. On the first night we went to a show of Japanese arts including the tea ceremony.

During the day we visited the gardens in Nara and at that time there were masses of rhododendrons and azaleas in flower. The effect was spectacular and the memory has remained with me ever since.

On our last day we drove from Kyoto, which is the religious capital of Japan, to Nara where I was very impressed by the Shinto shrines. In the evenings we went out with our interpreter-guide, she was very Westernised but provided a valuable bridge between our respective cultures. We got quite used to eating sitting on the ground. I got hooked on sake, the famous rice wine and also on Kobe beef, which must be very expensive to produce as the meat to be eaten is apparently massaged on the hoof.

In Tokyo we went everywhere by underground and got used to reading the Japanese signs. The underground is not nearly as frightening as it appears on films, which always seem to be made at the height of the rush hour.

(d) Formosa etc.

My next visit to the Far East took us to Formosa where my eldest son was running American Express. He had a large first floor flat where we stayed and on the Sunday of our visit he took us for a drive over the hills to the beach where there are the most extraordinary sandstone forms that have been thrown up by the effect of sea water and wind.

The real high point of my trip to Formosa was the underground museum, where they have all the treasures from the Winter Palace, brilliantly shipped under the supervision of an Australian and with the help of Chiang Kai-Shek's Army to Formosa to escape the Chinese. Obviously only a small part can be on show at any time but the richness of what was there was quite stunning and I would like to have spent much longer in the museum than we did.

Back in Hong Kong we mainly did our shopping in Kowloon where there are shops full of goods from Shanghai, many made out of jade, which are extraordinarily cheap. On that trip we went on to the beautiful island of Bali which we loved and where the people were so welcoming and gentle.

On the way home we stopped in Tahiti to visit one of the smaller islands, which was fun but also the most expensive part of our journey. Tahiti itself is a tourist hell and I would no more go back there than I would go to Kings Cross. The timings of our flights meant we had to spend one night but we ate in the hotel rather than sample its delights.

(e) The Iberian Peninsula

A great friend of ours had a house in a village on the coast just south of Lagoa where we spent many happy holidays, considerably enhanced by the lovely swimming pool. Or if we wanted a change there was marvellous beach which one approached through caves in the cliffs which had no doubt been used for smugglers. On the local beach you could get sardines for lunch. Apart from sardines, in Lagoa there is a marvellous local way of grilling squid.

At that part of the Atlantic the water tends to be quite cold but with brilliant sun, although this is not a disadvantage. My eldest step-daughter and her husband have a house about fifty miles north of Seville in the province of that name. It was an old olive-producing farm with a mill and lots of Ali-Baba jars to hold the oil. My late wife and I visited them frequently and spent many happy times there.

I remember one year travelling with them and their two very small children for a family holiday in Corfu. We rented a villa near the beach and a car. Corfu town itself is very colourful, although is now starting to get overrun by tourists. We were told that the local plane disgorges four hundred passengers three times an hour. I frightened myself one day, driving to the top of the hill where there is a particularly fine monastery. There was a succession of hairpin bends covered with loose gravel on which one tended to skid. I do not have a good head for heights at the best of time, except when I've got skis on so the whole experience was rather nerve-wracking!

(f) Italy

In 1985, with my father at the wheel, my wife, my stepmother and I set out in the large Fiat estate car from Isola Farnese. An hour and a half later following the Autostrada up the course of the Tiber we arrived outside Orvieto, and stopped for liquid refreshments in the car. Drivers were changed after 40 minutes.

At the top of the escarpment, spurning the road to the Duomo, in search of the Morino restaurant Father negotiated a maze of narrow streets until a bend north of the Duomo proved too tight and a hospitable parking spot within 3 minutes walk appeared and was seized immediately.

The façade was as stunning as its descriptions; the interior, blessedly uncluttered, was far superior.

Apart from the majesty of conception the great attraction was the Chapel of the Madonna di San Brizio whose walls are covered in frescos superbly preserved. Fra

Angelico having completed two panels, got called away to Roma, leaving Signorelli to complete his masterpiece. The latter put them both in black robes, in a corner of the picture, a picture, which inspired Michaelangelo's Sistine chapel.

Opposite is the chapel of the 'Corporal' commemorating a miracle in 1263 which led to the establishment of the feast of 'Corpus Christi'.

An enormous fine reliquary contains the corporal on which a drop of blood was seen to fall from the host that day in Balsena. There is also a lovely Madonna by Lippo Memmi, but the frescos are not memorable and, because we had no 100 lire piece, remained unlit.

In the town, between showers, a large number of young men in blue uniforms, resembling air force cadets, hurried about, most of them with a girl on their arms, suggesting a local barracks.

Several narrow lanes and a couple of wrong turnings later we arrived on foot at the Morino. Originally it was no doubt called after the moor, who strikes the bell on the clock tower to the left of the cathedral. Their own brand of Orvieto and then superloo, although both excellent, did not outweigh a rather average meal, nor justify a Michelin star and a price commensurate.

The owner's frequent cries of 'benissime' gave an impression of good service which was not always fully maintained. I, scorning the offer of an umbrella, hurried off to retrieve the car, getting deservedly damp for my pains.

By 2.45.p.m. we were rolling back to the motorway and some 75 minutes later trying to find out which part of Arezzo's ubiquitous Vice Garibaldi we had hit. Ignoring helpful, but misleading advice, I eventually located the given circle on which the Continental sits.

Just before six we set out on foot for San Francesco, a lofty great barn of a church famous for its frescos by Piero della Francesca in the choir. The state of preservation is disappointing and the lighting, for which we paid L100, inadequate, so that I was much less impressed by these than the Orvieto frescos. Nevertheless they are very fine, but being contemporaneous with those of Fra Angelico they look slightly more primitive.

Up the hill, crowded to the side of the road by a stinking diesel bus, just beyond the Post Office a road to the right reveals the campanile of Santa Maria della Pieve. As we approach it grows in charm until the full façade is seen with it 68 different pillars dating from the 11th century.

Inside the church is massively impressive. Digging in the crypt, for the foundations of the temple of Boccha, no doubt, has led to a reconstruction of the top end of the church in the last century which mars its simplicity.

At this point Father felt that he had had his fill for the day. He and Kay returned to the hotel and I climbed to the gardens at the top of the town. A marble mess commemorates Petrarch, and beyond there is a fine panorama of Tuscany which only requires that we ignore modern development in the foreground. To the left the Duomo has an ugly campanile, built around 1859. The main part of the cathedral is 5 centuries old and has a fine interior. On the left in a chapel with some excellent Della Robbias, but, with mass having started, these had to be left for later.

The upper part of Arezzo has been well preserved as a medieval city: if only the fumes of diesel buses could be banned!

After a rest we returned to San Francesco, this time to visit the Buca, a cellar in which excellent food and wines are served by a very helpful staff, and at 2/3 the price of lunch. The coffee machine had broken down, and we had to explain that it is possible to make coffee with boiling water instead of steam!

The fourth of May was a day of high cloud, the sun hiding until the middle of the afternoon.

Half an hour's drive brought us to the outskirts of Monterchi (3 km off the road to San Sepulchro). Beyond the town to the left is the cemetery with a small chapel on the right where I expected to see some rather gloomy Madonna.

Instead, over the altar of this fine white chapel, was a glorious painting of a fine pregnant medieval woman, her buttons strained and popping, flanked by angels, all in outstanding colours. Seldom has a detour been more worthwhile, and how poor are all reproductions seen to date.

About half an hour later we were parked opposite the Cathedral of San Sepulchro. The duomo itself has one lovely fresco by the door by a pupil of Piero della Francesca.

But in the Pinacotecha is Piero's glorious Resurrection and what a pair it makes with his pregnant Madonna! His fine altarpiece on the right is overshadowed by it. There is an excellent Della Robbia in the far hall and a couple of Signorellis, but the Pinacotecha belongs to the Resurrection.

An excellent hotel, outside on the road to Urbino, provided an impeccable lunch at a very reasonable price, no wonder it was full.

By 2.15.p.m. we were rolling up the winding but well marked road to Urbino. Over an hour later we saw this great little city extending up the mountainside. Approaching from behind we stopped to admire the view, then drove over the brow to the front of the palace and climbed up to the central square.

The outside courtyard has lost its Dalmation limestone facing on all but one wall. One side is flanked by a bare white cathedral, enriched by two fine baroque chapels. Coming through the entrance one is met by a perfect courtyard. To the left a fine wide, shallow-stepped, balustraded stairway leads up to the first floor. At once one feels that this is how we should be coming to a ball, and that we are under dressed. The corridors round the palace are being restored and we go straight into a fine banqueting hall with two noble chimney pieces, fixed with decorative tiles and a vaulted ceiling of perfect proportion. Throughout the palace the rooms have a perfection of proportion, beautiful inlaid doors and a variety of floors and ceilings. Because certain rooms are closed as well as the parochial church, there are too many works of art in the remaining rooms. All the works are of the XVth century or earlier. One must avoid indigestion and concentrate on the best, a feast in themselves. Despite all the beauties of paintings by Venocchio, Flemish masters Della Franchesca and Raphael's father, the most striking is probable the profile of Frederico Montefeltio, Duke of Urbino and creator of all this beauty with his son Guidobaldo.

And so to Rimini; a cross between Brighton, Saint Juan les Pins and Blackpool. Our hotel was The Grand, very like a Brighton hotel near the front and pleasantly furnished in modern style. The restaurant was closed so a short walk, not to the Michelin star restaurant but to the one recommended to Father by the receptionist. And what a good recommendation, charming service and very good food, particularly the grilled seafood.

Up betimes to get the car fixed of its smells of exhaust and rubber. We located a Fiat agent in the 'Saint Jean les Pins' district 15 minutes away and a short test satisfied him that the rubber smell was the clutch. Once up on the hoist, the holes in the silencer clearly showed where the exhaust fumes were escaping.

They had a spare and fixed it all in an hour for about £8. Full marks.

Xandra and I had to see the Malatesta Temple (in fact a church) but built to the greater glory of Sigi Somondo and his third wife Isolta (he murdered the second) rather than God.

War damage has been well repaired and the interior was most rewarding for the imaginativeness of the decoration. Columns based on twin elephants (Malatesta beasts) and marble reliefs on the right of the signs of the zodiac and on the left of numerous 'putti' playing. The little boy and girl in the sea were delightful.

Just over an hour's drive, across the Rubicon, saw us in Ravenna. Although the outskirts have little advantage over those of Rimini, the centre of town has been well preserved and is a basically Roman Town. Not for nothing is this area called the 'Romagna'. We stayed at the 'Jolly' Hotel which was modest modern and comfortable and the lunch quite good. After a siesta, we started on St Vitalio, the greatest of the churches with the finest mosaics. After 1400 years, the pictures look like this year's story book for children; particularly Abraham giving some bread to three angels, sitting at table with beautiful manners, while poor Isaac lies there awaiting the chop. Placidia's mausoleum could be out of the same book only the colours seem to be even more vivid.

After the feast I expected Father to have had his fill. Not at all; off we went to St Appolinaris in Classe (the small village 3k out of town which used to be the port). We were rewarded by a lovely classic church built on Roman lines, but most of the mosaics, sadly, were behind scaffolding. Then to the Cathedral tapestry which was suitably rewarding with mosaics of Christ in the Jordan and finally to St Appolinaris la miova which looked pretty old and where I was scandalised at being charged for admittance (the church still being in use on Sunday). The mosaics here were excellent, the long queues of virgins one side and of martyrs the other being particularly memorable.

A last, a good Italian dinner and early to bed. Everybody surprisingly made 10.30 Mass in the church opposite, a fine building in its own right but heavily restored. Memorable perhaps for four *girl* acolytes, although the priest was flanked by a boy on either side.

And so back to Rome or on the Venice as the case might be.

Dermot's first wife Patricia.

Endpiece

It is certainly true that 'One man in his time plays many parts'. In my case I have always tried to give what the parts demanded. In truth I always enjoyed playing the part of chairman most and was probably better prepared for that than any of the other many parts I have played.

I am aware that I failed my first wife, but have not wished to go into detail here. I was lucky enough to receive her forgiveness before she died. As a father I have succeeded in enjoying many sailing and skiing holidays with my children and they have all grown up to be affectionate and helpful individuals, so I do not feel I can have been too bad a father.

In all, mine has been a most interesting and rewarding life, for which I am grateful and I hope my successors are fortunate enough to enjoy theirs as much as I have mine.

Grandchildren, left to right, Laura, Kate, Mark, Toby, Ed, Isabelle, Freddie, Christopher.

Index

Amery, Julian 27
Antigua 8

Balingal, Gus 57
Beaulieu 104
Bell, Dom Maurice 49
Berger, Roland 96, 99
Bey, Zia 62, 67
Bowker, Jim and Elsa 19

Cadbury Committee 89
Calor Gas 81, 84-85, 87, 141
Canada 27-28, 34, 38
Chaplin, Jacky 10, 23, 111
Chaplin, Reginald 10
Cicele de Trafford 4
CompAir 88-89
Cowes 112
Cowfold, Sussex 22

de Massy, Henry 1, 6
de Massy, Richard 1
de Massy, Robert 1, 6
de Massy, Sir Hammo 1
De Trafford, June 20, 40
de Trafford, Rudolph 19-20, 151, 153, 156
de Trafford, Sir Humphrey 6
de Trafford, Sir Thomas Joseph 4
de Trafford, Xandra 151, 156

Demeure, Adolph 83, 84
Dunsmuir family 9, 10

Éclair 114
Egerton House 48

Formosa 150
Franklin, Violet Maud 6

Galopin, Genevieve 39
Geoffrey Chapman Ltd 91
Greece 71-80

Harrow 52-55
Hungary 98

Iberian Peninsula 150
Illingworth, John 114-115
Italy 151-157

Jameson, Joan 11-12
Jameson, Shane 20, 45, 46, 52
Jameson, Tommy 11-12, 24
Japan 148-149
Jeanne 104, 110, 112
Jessel, Charles 20-21, 40, 42
Jessel, George 40, 42
Jessel, Muriel 43
Johnson, Charlie 19

Kayak 112

Kent 20-21, 40
Klosters 144

Lagos 86, 87
Le Rosey 51
Leningrad 97
Low and Bonar 86

Magnier, Clem 111
Menzies, Violet and Keith 25
Moscow 96-97
Mouse of Malham 115
Musgrave, Dorothy 11
Musgrave, Sir Richard and Lady 11-12
Myth of Malham 114

O'Brien, Johnny 45
O'Leary, Bernard 61
Odile 141
Okosi, Anne 38

Pandos, Laura 76
Parisbas Ltd 82
Petrofina 85
Pilkington family 6
Powell, Enoch 101

Ralph 1, 6

Skagerrak 116-141
SOAS London University 55
South America 147

Talbot, John 4
Toombs, Bill 67
Trafford Park 2, 4, 6
Trafford, Randolph, Lord of 1
Trafford, Sir Cecil 2
Trafford, Sir John 1
Triarch 116
Turkey 56-70

USA 146

Walsh, Paddy 44
Warburgs 81
Waterford 20-21, 43
Wilson, Harold 103
Wilson, Sandy 54-55
Worth Priory 48, 49, 51
Wulstan-Philipson, Dom 48-49

Zermatt 115